INTRODUCTION

Since modern, recorded Golf began in 1457, give or take, golf teaching and learning has obviously been a big part of the game. Throughout the ensuing years it has developed into what it is today. We have followed a path which came about as a result of our own logical thinking and method of problem solving, which has been subsequently backed up by scientific analysis and data. Also, we both copy and listen to the Top players and their advice, and their own perception of what they believe has gone towards making them successful.

In this book we add an extra ingredient into the mix, a knowledge of the subconscious mind, and immediately our current methods come into question. We are completely unaware of our subconscious mind, because it is just that, subconscious. However, we do know that it controls so much of our lives, and above everything, 'all of our movement.'

Our present methods of learning, are mostly based around a mechanical understanding of the golfswing, and with very little acknowledgment of the workings within our own individual subconscious mind.

Are we really learning in a way that is both

compatible, and fully exploiting, our own subconscious mind?

In this book, we not only ask this question, but we also offer an alternative pathway, which has already begun to show some extraordinary results.

'Rocking the Fairways' has come about as a result of having to fix my own game, which had deteriorated to such an extent that it had looked completely beyond repair. In this case, the success has been born out of the failure, and arguably a more in depth understanding has evolved.

ROCKING
THE
FAIRWAYS

BY

RICHARD FISH

This book is dedicated to my family and all those that search the real truth.

Richard Fish. European Tour player 1978-1990.

CONTENTS

THE PLAYERS

Author: *Richard Fish*

Caddy: *Oliver Sellen*

Cover Art: *Miki de Goodaboom*

PART ONE

ON THE FIRST
SUBCONSCIOUS GOLF

In which the Rtf foundation is laid.

Generally speaking, we know little or nothing of the subconscious, because it is just that, sub-conscious; beneath our conscious. So, assuming at least a basic level of understanding of golf, let's explore the subconscious, and see if we can make any connections between the two.

And so, to begin with, if we break the mind down into conscious and subconscious, we could see the whole thing as an iceberg with the tip which we see being the conscious, and that which is below water is the subconscious. In essence, the conscious is all of the thoughts of which we are aware, and the subconscious, all those of which we know nothing: with thoughts flowing between the two all the time. And if we look just at the subconscious, we could see it as a perfect natural computer. The subconscious holds a record of everything we've ever experienced, which in itself is utterly extraordinary, but what makes it even better than this is that it also has a fantastic operating system which retrieves required information, in a timely manner. The subconscious drives all of our bodily systems and also our movement, and so here we have our first connection with golf; it's a moving thing. So, the subconscious actually operates exactly as a computer: a natural computer, and fortunately one which requires no upgrades.

Now, what we need to really get to grips with, with our natural computer, is the 'programmer', being the single most critical element, which *Rff* refers to as Mr Sensitive. 'He' is the link between the conscious and subconscious, and effectively has his finger on the pulse of our mind. 'His' function is that of a radar system, scanning our environment, and feeding all the information it's receiving into the computer for processing. Sometimes we will need to act on the information immediately, and other times the information will be stored and held for later use: or if deemed insignificant, my understanding is that it is effectively deleted or at least held in the deepest and most inactive part of the subconscious, as opposed to the stuff we need, which will be held close to hand. An example of immediate use of incoming information would be shown in our Fight or Flight response; our decision is immediate and we do one or the other; it's our essential survival system. And an example of information held for later could be course conditions we're facing, which will be used in our consideration of our next shot; so here's a second connection.

In *Rtf* this function is referred to as Mr Sensitive, simply because the level of sensitivity 'he' detects is mind boggling, detecting not only the blunt stuff as in Fight or Flight, but also minute changes in mood, all the way through to intuition and our Sixth Sense; so, Mr Sensitive is completely appropriate, though we could even go a little further. Not only does he have this incredible sensitivity, he has much more, is much more, than just this. He is effectively our conductor, taking all the information in, and then, working with the rest of the subconscious, influences and guides our next thoughts and actions: in short, he's the Man. 'He' is the regulator and moderator of all thought flows between the conscious and subconscious, and if he likes a proposed response from the subconscious he'll go with it, but if not, it ain't going to happen; he decides. He runs the operating system and part of his work is that he regulates and prioritises how information is stored and processed in our subconscious, and as such, is our subconscious computer programmer. Understanding his function is absolutely fundamental to acquiring a full understanding of *Rtf*: in short, everything we do automatically, such as eating, driving, walking and so on, is driven by subconscious programs which have been laid down over time; often as children, though obviously not driving.

Now, Subconscious Golf has been around for a long time. Indeed all good golfers have always played Subconscious Golf, meaning that from the moment the backswing begins, the conscious is switched off, and the subconscious takes over, until the moment they look up to watch the flight of the ball. This has happened, and would happen, absolutely irrespective of anyone ever having studied and or written about this aspect of golf. Old Tom Morris did it, and so did Joyce Wethered; they all did. It's the only way to get the ball from A to B effectively: so here's a further connection made. So while the study of the subconscious, in golfing terms, came about around the seventies, don't think that it didn't exist before then – it did. The same as birds could always fly whether or not man had studied the subject. And the studies to date have been pretty sporadic, with every now and again someone making a further contribution to this field of knowledge. Google research into the subject shows that there have been various variations on the theme, but it certainly appears, given it is a critical area when considering improving our game, that the theory has gained little overall traction in practice, and we can conclude that as yet it is having only limited application; Subconscious Golf, it would appear, is yet in its infancy.

And now's the time to pull Old Tom Morris and Mr Sensitive together. In order to hit our 'perfect' shot, we need to have practiced it enough for Mr Sensitive to have programmed our computer, referred to in the book as Mr Computer. All the practice shots have been recorded in the subconscious, and come the moment, the subconscious is able to recreate the shot from the program which is already there. Now, whether the shot is based exactly on the program of the best practice shot, or the shot is based on a variation of the best practice shot, is a debatable point. In reality it is probably a mix of the two: the essential program is there, but it's likely, given the almost infinite ability of the subconscious, it's actually adapted in real time to suit the given conditions, with every single shot being different. This understanding is probably fairly close to the reality. Therefore, to achieve the 'perfect' shot for the occasion, the program must flow freely to drive our physical movement. The required process, in short, is this. Our conscious, when considering our next shot, is loading up what it deems to be the necessary information, such as wind speed, club choice, distance required, ball flight required, and so on. And as Mr Sensitive regulates this incoming information, a program is loading up in the subconscious. And if Mr Sensitive is happy with the proposed program that he's monitoring as it's loading, he'll step aside as the backswing begins, and allow the swing to be produced from the subconscious program. And in this scenario, where the conscious and subconscious are perfectly aligned, thanks to the work of Mr Sensitive, Old Tom Morris and Joyce Wethered hit their 'perfect' shots. And so can we. I hope by now we're beginning to see that the links between the subconscious and golf are becoming fairly apparent, and well worth our time exploring, which is what this book is all about.

In our everyday lives, we know nothing of, and are completely unaware of our subconscious and just how much it is doing for us all the time. All our physical movements are carried out on autopilot, perfectly. Just try doing any everyday activity using only your conscious; it's actually impossible in reality. And the point is this: if it works so well everywhere else, without any maintenance whatsoever, why wouldn't we use it in our golfswing? And for this process, the swing, we could see the subconscious as the surgeon's knife, with the conscious being a lump hammer; choose your weapon, and choose wisely.

ON THE SECOND
JOHN'S STORY

*In which we look at the story of one of my pupils, this being
an example of Rtf thinking in action.*

At the beginning of *Rtf*, around five years ago, I needed to have some students that might be interested to try this new way of way of thinking, that on face value might appear to be somewhat radical, or certainly different at least. I knew the ideas were good, but I wanted to find out just how good they really were, when put into practice. My first two 'volunteers', were John and Clayton. I am happy to say that their success has comfortably surpassed anything that both myself and the pair of them could have possibly hoped for, and they are still continuing to improve further, even today. This is John's story.

I might have been lucky with John, it's hard to know, but his improvement has been unbelievable. I may even be tempted to claim, the likes of which have never been seen before. Probably what's even harder to grasp, is that John doesn't really make that much of an effort, and I could easily see him improving much more. I might have considered it a bit of a fluke, except that Clayton has had exactly the same experience, equally as dramatic, and also with relatively little effort.

John was sixty-six years old, had been playing for thirty years, and was playing off fifteen handicap, which was as low as he'd ever managed to achieve. I hope he won't mind me saying, but his ball striking was awful, even for a fifteen handicap standard, but he actually had a pretty good short game.

I played with him for about three years before I started coaching him. I used to play a lot with him and a South African Senior tour player, who used to play with John almost every day, whilst also coaching him. It would have to be said, that everything John had been taught at that time would have been under the umbrella of traditional teaching, and John was a very traditional thinker, and had never questioned or doubted anything that he'd so far learned. He was delighted and grateful to be receiving so much attention from such a prestigious coach and player, and why shouldn't he! However, John had never shown any signs of improvement, and even some deterioration, despite playing so much golf. This didn't seem totally strange, as John was sixty-six years old and had assumed it was the downward spiral that comes with aging, which many of us have grudgingly had to accept. He had also accepted that this was his level of ability, and couldn't expect a lot more. However, this didn't help his level of frustration, and John suffered very badly with this.

He was a typical amateur and came right over the top – swung across the ball – and always finished standing on his right foot. He feared hitting it to the right but could easily hit it miles left as well. He appeared to pick the club up on the backswing, with very little turn; his swing was certainly no thing of beauty, and I've rarely seen a person suffer with quite as much inconsistency. Understandably, his inner confidence could really plummet quickly and dramatically.

Before I was coaching him, he went to a local custom fitting guru to be fitted for a new driver. The guru was well respected locally, and some tour players often used him. I remember that the driver cost a small fortune and John couldn't wait to put it into action. As soon as I saw his new driver, my reservations began immediately, but of course I said nothing. However, just as I suspected, his driving became significantly worse, which was less than ideal as this was easily, already the worst part of John's game. It was very clear that the driver had been fitted using the feedback of the statistics derived from the Launch monitor and nothing else. John did hit the ball very high, and he therefore had been fitted with an 8.5 degree, stiff-shafted driver. Unfortunately, he hadn't learned anything about John himself, or his golfswing, and neither did he understand how our subconscious mind works. These three things would surely have to come first in any custom fit or golf lesson, well before you'd even consider using technical statistics, would you agree? At that time, experiences like this helped me to firmly push on with my own thinking and experimentation, because I wasn't liking the way the industry was moving, where commercialism was at the forefront, and high-tech gadgetry was dominating and selling golf lessons. For me the understanding of the person and the mind had to come before anything else. Either way, the result of this fitting became fascinating for me about three years later.

Anyway, the South African pro decided to return to South Africa and suddenly John was coachless. In the beginning, I wasn't sure about coaching John, because he didn't appear to want to change from thinking traditionally, and neither was I prepared to compromise my beliefs for the sake of giving him something that he thought he needed.

The first step came when John used to ask me what he had done wrong every time he hit a bad shot. I turned to him one day and said, 'Did you make the swing that you had originally planned and intended?'

'No, of course not,' he replied.

'Then why would you expect to hit a good shot?' I replied.

I went on to explain. 'You wouldn't make a wild slash at tennis or any other sport, and expect the ball to drop just inside the baseline, as you had intended, now would you?'

He managed to see the sense in what I was saying. I asked him if he could show me how he had meant to swing. On a practice swing, he could do this with ease, and made a decent looking swing.

'Okay,' I said, 'if you swing nicely and still hit a bad shot, then come to me, but in the meantime, do you not think that you have a responsibility to at least do as you had originally intended and make a reasonable swing at least?'

From this point onwards, John began to understand the relationship between a good movement – swing – and a good shot. A good movement may not guarantee a good shot, but it would likely improve the odds dramatically. John began to show his first signs of improvement, but there was a long way to go.

The next step was when John talked to me about his problem of coming across the ball, or what we call coming over the top. He had spent a good few years trying to cure this problem, with lots of professional advice, but to no avail: he wasn't even slightly better.

He talked to me about this. I asked him why coming over the top was always seen as a fault. I didn't necessarily see it this way at all. I went on to explain how it can actually be a working and effective way of playing golf. All he had to do was to understand that it was likely to produce a fade – when he hit a good shot – and this was the shot that he should picture. It was a little like playing table tennis and only playing with slice; it works just fine and can be a very consistent way of playing. This doesn't mean that he can't learn to hit a top spin forehand later, but for now he could have a working and consistent way of playing. I told him to picture this shot and then as long as he was able to make a coordinated and balanced swing, there was every chance that he would hit a great shot! His first little bit of improvement.

At this point, I wasn't really John's coach, but I was certainly starting to get his ear, when the next significant event happened. One day we were playing, and John was in the middle of having one of his really bad days. Eventually the frustration became too much for him and he needed to talk about it. He went on to explain to me just how nervous and uptight he was on every tee shot. I did empathise with him, but this wasn't the moment for sympathy. I asked him what kind of driver of the ball he saw himself as; consistent, inconsistent, or very inconsistent. He immediately replied, 'Very inconsistent.'

I then asked him, if he thought that it was a perfectly reasonable response that his mind was clearly panicking, whilst standing on the tee, bearing in mind this information.

'Well yes, I suppose it is,' he replied. All of a sudden John had established a starting point. He had accepted that he was a very inconsistent driver of the ball. I explained to him that he was not admitting defeat, but was merely recognising where he is now, and now it's time to do something about it. He agreed, and suddenly, at that moment, I became John's coach.

I explained a little about how the mind works, and the first thing that we need to do is find a way to lower the degree of difficulty, and help to calm and gain a little more harmony within his subconscious mind. I persuaded John to look for, and try out, a driver with a lot more loft and possibly a softer shaft. He wasn't sure, because he was concerned about hitting the ball too high. I went on to explain how the increase in backspin could help him to hit the ball straighter, strike the ball better, and how making life easier would be such a good thing to bring his tension levels down, at least for now. He ended up with a new driver that had 12 degrees of loft and a regular shaft.

John now had an easier club to play with, and he also knew that he was trying to make a great swing, with its connection to better shots. Suddenly Mr Sensitive was more trusting of the situation, and was beginning to allow him to swing with the fluid coordination that he was more than capable of. John made his next bit of improvement and we were on our way.

It wasn't long before John wanted to move on and improve even more. He was still not satisfied and he wasn't particularly keen on fading the ball. That was fine by me, because I also knew that John was capable of a lot more.

I had realised, like many others, that coming over the top, or swinging across the ball, was just John's own interpretation of trying to hit a straight shot. This was simply his own personal reaction when trying to hit the ball straight, stand straight, and swing on line. Put simply, he wasn't very good at it. However, on the other hand, did he really have to be? Personally I didn't think so. I wouldn't imagine that Bubba Watson is particularly good at hitting a straight shot, and neither are many great players, but that certainly doesn't make them bad either. Some people just don't see 'straight' very easily, and our coaching system doesn't cater particularly well for these people.

I started by asking John if he could hit a fade, which of course he could do easily. I then asked him if he thought he could manage to hit a draw as well. I first explained that there were no rules of how he should stand, align himself, grip, the angle of his clubface, swing, or anything. The only rule was that the ball had to start out to the right, as a ball that starts straight and then hooks, is of no use to anyone.

I explained to him, that above anything else, he had to picture the ball starting out to the right of target. I then asked him what direction he thought that the club should swing on, and he could easily understand how the clubhead had to be swinging from in to out to create the shot that he wanted. He then took a practice swing and on his first attempt showed me a swing that looked absolutely ideal for hitting a lovely draw. He was instantly ready to make his first real attempt with the ball.

John wasn't brilliant at doing this at first, but he wasn't terrible either, and could at least make a passable attempt with different degrees of success. There was no reason to expect him to be great at it either; Mr Computer had not been fully programmed as yet, and Mr Sensitive knew this, so John naturally found it difficult to properly coordinate or trust his swing from the beginning. However, he already had a pretty good idea of what he was at least trying to do, all done without one single mechanical swing thought, or any positional instruction from me. He had worked it all out for himself, just from me explaining what he was trying to do with the ball, and explaining that there were no rules as to how he could achieve what he wanted to. So, he now had a game with a few working principles.

He knew that if he made a decent coordinated movement at the ball, the result was likely to be reasonable, and certainly much better than if he didn't.

He had learned the feel of hitting a fade and a draw, and understood that a straight shot was somewhere in between the two, which he could now achieve with a bit of visualisation with no need to become overly fixated on everything being perfectly straight or square, as he had once thought.

He had now built up a much improved sense of the direction of his hit, where he knew how not coming over the top felt, because he was now capable of starting the ball out to the right and hitting a draw, which he couldn't possibly do if he had come over the top.

John had previously been very handicapped by the industry. He was playing golf under a set of rules that he thought that he was supposed to adhere to. He thought he should stand square and the clubface had to be square, takeaway correct, and so much more. I showed him how so many of these so-called rules were actually so full of contradiction. I also told him that he no longer had to abide by them either. He didn't have to stand square, he didn't have to have the clubface square, and he no longer needed to think of his swing mechanically. *In fact he no longer had any rules whatsoever and could make up a whole new set if he wanted, and ones that would be completely designed around him and his needs.* This helped a lot, but it is amazing how conditioned we all are, and it took a long time before John had the confidence to move completely away from the perceived and false safety of the textbook and convention.

He also no longer had to do everything being square and straight. It is so much easier to be somewhere a little bit under or over, as opposed to being exactly in the middle. Once you get the feeling for 'either side', it's easy to find where somewhere in the middle is. All of this became the equivalent of taking off an invisible straightjacket: John was now free and his golfswing began to show it too.

Despite learning to fade and draw, John opted more and more for a straight shot when he was playing, and was now considerably better at it. Practicing the fade and draw had clearly given John a much better feeling for hitting the ball straight, and he now found it relatively easy, especially as he wasn't governed by 'mechanically' aiming straight, and had lost that feeling of trying to control everything exactly. However, he was also able to use his fade or draw on certain holes, if he felt it would make the task a little easier.

The next stage was when I began to explain to John how his subconscious mind was working. He began to develop a much better understanding of why he sometimes missed and how he could get in his own way at times. He was also able to see the circumstances that were likely to lead up to a good shot, and equally the circumstances that would lead up to a bad shot. This understanding started to make golf less frustrating and much more understandable for him, plus he could now see how he could make things better too. He was now in full swing with the One Shot Theory (chapter ten) and finding ways to lower the degree of difficulty. John was starting to improve the dialogue that was going on in his mind, and was sometimes able to calm Mr Sensitive where it would previously have been impossible.

John could feel he was improving and this momentum was firmly in his favour, and there was no real reason why this was likely to change. He had left behind his former culture where he would learn a new swing and then be permanently in fear that he could suddenly lose it: which he always did, of course. Now he had nothing to lose, his swing was entirely natural. He could have a bad day or bad hole, but he could never lose his swing: there was nothing to lose, it was simply his own natural subconscious reaction to the circumstances he had provided.

Strange things happened along the way that I could never have foreseen. John's 12 degree driver, which he had learned to love and trust, broke one day. He was absolutely devastated. Anyway, he happened to find another one, which was the same make and type, but had 9 degrees of loft and a firm shaft. It was cheap and in a sale, and he bought it on impulse. Amazingly he hit this new driver superbly and longer than his previous one. Suddenly he now had a driver that was pretty similar to the one that he'd been fitted for and wasn't able to hit, only this one he hit fantastically. It wasn't difficult for me to see what had happened, or at least partially, as I had been watching his progress all the way. If John had tried this new driver three years earlier, he wouldn't have been able to hit it, and yet now he could hit it beautifully. Over time, John's stress levels had considerably lowered and his swing was becoming more and more fluid and coordinated, from one day to the next. He had developed into a whole different player and now was beginning to have an elegant-looking swing, and already he was capable of doing all kinds of things that would have previously been impossible.

That's just about it. Anything else would have been personal to John and not especially relevant. I have always been there for him as a coach and mentor, but so much of his journey has been about his own self-discovery.

He has moved entirely away from thinking positionally in his golfswing. On a bad day, he often tells me how he becomes 'aware' of his backswing.

He now hits the ball beautifully; he is quite long, and bizarrely getting longer, and at times could almost be mistaken for a Senior tour player, himself. He really is capable of hitting it superbly off the tee. Unquestionably he has reached a standard that I would never have thought possible: and he's still getting better.

Interestingly, it has been quite a while since I first wrote this, and John has improved so much in just that space of time. He is now sixty-nine, and is very comfortably playing to a 9 handicap and he now gets thirty-four points on a not-so-good day. John and all of my pupils surprise me almost every day. I can't believe how much they continue to improve without mechanical changes and with so little input from me. John has improved beyond a level that anyone would have thought possible, but still amazingly looks like he could easily improve much more.

PART TWO

ON THE THIRD
THE BASICS

In which we attempt to establish a reliable foundation on which we can build our best game. That this foundation should contain the essential elements of a great player's game is probably a given: but what are the essentials of Golf: what are the real Basics?

It doesn't matter what it is we are trying to learn, our instructor often tells us just how important it is to get the basics right first. I'm sure that I've said this myself and have also heard many other golf coaches often stressing the importance of the basics. This is not just applied to beginners either, as I've often heard coaches telling experienced players who are having troubles, to, 'Go back to the basics.'

It seems reasonable that we should all be taught the Basics: after all, we would all like to know what is required, and hence what we are at least trying to do, in order to hit a great golf shot. In this chapter, I'd like to raise the question, 'What are the real basics?'

First, before we attempt to find the answer to this, it's important that we establish the difference between a preference and a basic. A basic would surely have to be something that is common to *all* great ball strikers and connects all good shots, as opposed to a preference which would be something that might suit and help some players, but not others; a preference would be more personal to each individual. Not only this, but preferences change as we further develop, but the basics presumably are something that we will always be doing, just as long as we are striking the ball well.

It's important to make this distinction, because we mustn't fall into the trap of teaching someone a preference and labeling it as a basic, because we wouldn't want to limit somebody's potential by tying them up with something that doesn't suit them, and is not designed around their own very specific needs. I say this because this might be a trap that so many of us are unwittingly falling into and making golf unnecessarily too difficult for so many. My experience and belief is that this is happening much more than we may even think it does, and more than we even dare to imagine.

Okay, so let's try to find out what the basics really are. This way we should know what it is that we are all at least trying to achieve, and then we will be in a position to move on, and find our own set of individual preferences, that help us to perform at our best. So, we need to know what it is that connects all good shots and something that all good ball strikers do; anything that sits outside of this can only be deemed as a preference.

Immediately we can discount so much. Good players don't all stand square or aim straight. Neither do they all have the exact same ball position with a perfectly square clubface and textbook posture. They don't all swing it on plane, or consciously try to shift their weight to the right on the backswing, while turning their shoulders ninety degrees, or any of the swing positions that we are being told are 'essential.' This means that none of these things, and so much more that we often assume are essential for playing good golf, can be deemed as one of the basics.

There might be a few things that sit on the edge of being one of the basics, but on closer inspection fall short.

Possibly the one thing that most pros might agree on, is that good players all have a pretty decent grip, and this is key to hitting a good shot. I probably have a similar view here too, but even this is actually contradictory, because great players have all kinds of different grips. We can all have preferences with the grip, but we cannot teach one and the same grip, because we have not yet found a grip that we can be certain will suit everyone. In fact Mo Norman, who was widely thought of as the best ball striker ever, had a grip that completely bucked the trend, and was very personal to only him. Hopefully we can all agree that the grip is clearly important, but it is not something that all good players do the same: therefore we can add grip to the endless list above. However, we could potentially say that it could be deemed a basic, for you to find a grip that is best suited to you. Unfortunately, once again this is something we really have to discard, for the reason that your grip is likely to evolve and change over the years, as you learn more and more about yourself and discover the idiosyncrasies and natural tendencies that are a part of your own personal swing: which is exactly what so many of the greats have done. We cannot deny the importance of the grip, but I'm afraid, for the reasons given, it must fall under the umbrella of being a preference, and definitely not a basic.

Some people might argue that all good players have a great impact position, and that this is also a basic. Of course, this is chiefly true, but hopefully you agree that this is only a result of a set of circumstances, and no good player is ever likely to be trying to place himself in to a specific position at impact; it just happens! Either way, we know that many great players haven't given their impact position any thought whatsoever, and, for this reason, we cannot call this a Basic, and is more likely something that we never even have to think about. Besides, good shots come in all kinds of shapes and guises, and the vast majority of us couldn't hope to achieve some of these deemed classical positions, that may not suit us at all, and will have nothing to do with why we hit a good shot, or not. Therefore, a classic impact position is definitely not a basic.

Okay, bearing all this in mind, what is it that links all good shots?

The Rtf Basics

In my view, all good players have only one thing in common.

An ability to swing with fluid and coordinated

movement, which results in a fast, uninhibited, non-manipulated, swish of the clubhead at the point of impact.

The clubhead is also moving in a direction and at an angle, which is the result of an instinctive reaction that has been formed within the subconscious mind which corresponds directly to the type of shot that we are trying to hit. This will generally occur, as we find a set of circumstances that help us (Mr Sensitive) to be able to trust our ability to do the job.

Put simply, a free flowing swish at the point of contact with the ball is essential to achieve a great strike and the shot that you had intended. 'A free flowing swish is a result of good timing, as is good timing dependant on a free flowing swish.'

Yes, all great shots only occur when there is no attempt to steer or manipulate the clubhead, which could potentially lead to slowing it down. The easy way to picture this would be to try and imagine yourself striking a forehand drive at Squash or Racketball where an uninhibited, fast racket head will significantly improve the strike and eventually gain more control than a slow moving, manipulated, stiff, and controlled racket head: exactly the same applies to striking a golf ball.

While some people may argue that there are more things that might be common amongst good players, the only thing that links all good shots, is a free flowing, uninterrupted, non-manipulated, swishing clubhead. Therefore, for this reason, this is our one and only basic, and everything else has to be personal to each individual, and therefore a preference.

NB I'm talking about good shots, as opposed to some bad shots that are lucky enough to get a good result.

That's it! I hope you are not disappointed, but that really is it.

So, we now have our basics and they look absolutely nothing like any other set of basics that we have previously seen. Hopefully you can see my point though, and hopefully you agree with my assessment of basics compared to preferences, but how can we use this new found knowledge in any kind of positive way?

First, we can see that we are often taught the basics, which are in fact nothing more than preferences, which are clearly different from player to player. The danger of this is hopefully obvious to those of us who are obedient and follow instructions to the tee. There is no knowing just how difficult and limiting we could be making golf for so many people.

This leads nicely on to my next point, which suddenly becomes more obvious after our analysis of The Basics. The swinging of a golfclub is actually a pretty simple thing to do, despite what we are led to believe. All we have to do, is to create a well timed and coordinated swish of a clubhead in a direction that will propel the ball towards where we had intended. This sounds very different to the complicated set of instructions that us golfers usually grow up with.

Actually, I think it is fairly likely, after watching a few good players swing, that with our new set of Basics, most people could produce a fairly decent looking action very quickly, without the need for any of these complicated instructions; at least on a practice swing.

Therefore the next question has to be, 'So why don't we all swing and hit the ball well when we're playing?' A great question, and hopefully we're able to explain this more fully in the rest of this book.

In Short

All great players have only one thing, truly in common; the free flowing, well coordinated, and highly effective swing. We know that in order to produce this to the best of our ability, we need to both understand, and then apply our knowledge of the mind, and specifically the subconscious. This understanding leads us on to both mental and physical changes, but they are all based around our growing knowledge of the subconscious mind. And we're now on that path.

ON THE FOURTH
LOWERING THE DEGREE OF
DIFFICULTY

In which we look at the benefits of making the job easier,
and how this can have an effect on the way we swing.

Before we talk about the main subject in this chapter, I need to talk about something that is at the core of this whole book. Once we understand this, problem solving takes on a whole new dimension. This might be new knowledge to some of you, but this is certainly not new, and it is well known in the world of neuroscience.

All of our movement involves the larger, stronger muscles, which are supported by the smaller, more intricate muscles. While the big muscles are there for strength and power, it is the support of the smaller muscles that enables us to move with coordination and balance, and perform these impossibly complex tasks, of which, striking a golf ball is one.

The majority of these messages to the smaller muscles come from an area of the brain called the cerebellum. When the messages between the two are flowing freely, we are able to coordinate smoothly and easily. However, in certain situations, we can unwittingly sabotage this process, and fluid, coordinated, and balanced movement will then become very difficult. In short, when we have harmony within our mind, fluid movement is straightforward. When something happens that can upset this delicate balance, our movement will become increasingly clumsy and stiff. Hopefully, we can all clearly see how important this knowledge could potentially be if we are going to attempt something that requires the kind of intricacy and precision needed to strike a golf ball well.

For example, if we were to walk along a two-foot wide plank, while it was on the ground, we could all probably manage this easily, striding out confidently. However, if we began to raise this plank, we would begin to lose that confident stride. Our steps would become shorter, and we would probably have our arms outstretched on either side, counterbalancing ourselves, trying to maintain the balance that we once had, which has now become more difficult. This reflects the imbalance in our mind as we begin to doubt our ability to perform a task that we once thought was perfectly straightforward. If the plank was eventually raised to forty storeys high, we all would be left clutching on to the plank for dear life, too afraid to move, as none of us would be left with any possibility for any kind of fluid or balanced movement. Everything between the ground and forty storeys high would create varying degrees of discord within our mind, thus affecting our ability to move fluidly to varying degrees.

We could all probably see that if we lower the plank, movement will become easier, and if we raise it, movement will become more difficult and less fluid. Translate this over to golf, and we begin to understand the essence of this chapter, and how this could be essential information regarding our ability to learn and play the game.

In this book, I'm using Mr Sensitive (Mr S) and Mr Computer (Mr C) in order to make it easier for us to understand the subconscious mind. Mr C is the supercomputer that has all the information and ability to enable us to perform incredible tasks, moving with coordination and amazing levels of complexity. Whereas Mr S is our extremely sensitive warning system, and the one that gives the go ahead, or not, and all kinds of different levels between the two.

Therefore, and this is an important fact for the book, Mr C is the only one that can send out messages to the smaller muscles, giving us the ability to move with coordination, and therefore, any intrusion, or interference in his role, will make fluid movement more difficult. Okay, bearing this in mind, let's get on with lowering the degree of difficulty. And firstly, I'm hoping that you're able to accept the following two statements.

One: That any one of us can hit a good shot at any time, even if we are in a period of poor swinging. It doesn't matter if it is one in every hundred, or every other shot, the point is that we have all experienced the feeling of a coordinated swing that has resulted in a really good shot, at some time or other. This is your own definition of a good shot, relative to your own present capabilities, and is regardless of anyone else's opinion. In short, a shot and swing that you are really pleased with.

Two: Golf is a very difficult sport requiring incremental degrees of precision, together with very small margins of error, and where a bad shot can often be penalised very harshly, regardless of what level you are presently playing at.

Hopefully you agree with the above. So, bearing this in mind, there is a process that goes on within the subconscious mind of all golfers, on each and every shot. Mr S is permanently weighing up whether he is prepared to trust the program in the subconscious mind that Mr C is poised and ready to put into operation. Of course, if he is not able to trust this program, a poorly coordinated swing is likely to follow, as Mr C no longer has free rein, and the smaller muscles are no longer picking up clear signals.

Of course, each type of shot or situation in golf can be enormously different from one to the next, all requiring a different type of swing, or small variations in it, at least. For starters, we all have fourteen clubs to choose from, and each individual club can produce any number of different types of shots. There are different lies, situations, and course conditions. We will experience all kinds of varying weather conditions, different playing partners, and varying levels of tension, for all kinds of different reasons. If we were to list all the possible combinations of the above, it would probably add up to a figure that is well into the thousands. Who knows? The list is virtually endless. On each one of these occasions, Mr Sensitive is there deciding whether he is able to trust Mr Computer's program, which is uniquely designed for each individual specific shot and unique set of circumstances. In moments of doubt, sometimes our conscious mind may be able to persuade him to trust, and other times, there could be nothing that can talk him round. There are times when he may only be able to trust partially, and to all kinds of different degrees and levels.

It's quite difficult to imagine that we have so many different swings, and not just one for all occasions. As an example, try to imagine yourself walking. We all naturally assume that we always walk the same, using the same muscles and in the same way. Of course there are strong similarities, but this is not strictly true as we encounter different surfaces, inclines, bumps, and even weather conditions. The problem is that we manage to do this without any conscious thought, and we therefore tend to dismiss it as irrelevant, and assume we are doing the same thing every time we walk. If we were ever able to learn to walk on a clinically flat and firm surface, using only our conscious mind – which we couldn't do anyway – then we would certainly be completely scuppered if we suddenly encountered any irregularities that required a whole new set of calculations. Well, it's exactly the same in golf.

Anyway, we now know, that if Mr Sensitive is lacking trust, then fluid, coordinated movement will become more difficult as he begins to take control and interfere with the role of Mr Computer. We are likely to experience this in different ways, mostly depending on the varying levels of Mr Sensitive's trust, and the dialogue and harmony within our mind.

One way would be to feel like we have swung

without any coordination whatsoever, and we have completely lost balance, often with a feeling of 'coming up' and out of the shot, jerking or swinging too quickly. Afterwards, we would generally receive an unhelpful comment like:

'You lifted your head.'

'You swung too quickly.'

'You didn't complete your backswing.'

Or some other comment about the outer visual appearance which has happened as a result of us losing our ability to swing freely and with coordination. This is when Mr Sensitive has wanted to completely abort the swing, as his sense of danger exceeds his own comfort level.

Another way may feel like the clubhead is slowing up, and it becomes a physical effort to force the clubhead through. This is a similar sensation to when you become overly tense when throwing paper into a basket. Can you imagine yourself feeling like you are trying to steer or guide the screwed-up piece of paper into the basket? Can you imagine your arm feeling tense and your hand slowing down as it loses the ability for fluid and free-flowing movement? You still might succeed in throwing the paper into the basket, but the movement feels more inhibited. Well, we do exactly the same thing while playing golf.

Now, if we assume that a free-flowing, coordinated swing is what we would all like to achieve, the question becomes, how do we achieve this, and more importantly, how do we achieve it on a regular basis? Of course, good dialogue and harmony within our mind is something that we will always be responsible for, no matter what circumstances we find ourselves in. This will always give us our best chance to swing fluidly and as we had intended, as sometimes Mr Sensitive can be placated. Making clear, calm, and sensible decisions that we are able to commit to, will always help considerably, as this will feed Mr Computer with clear information, helping him to bring forth the best possible program, that Mr Sensitive is more likely to be comfortable with. And maintaining a quiet mind, and allowing our subconscious to complete the task without overly cluttering our mind with too many conscious thoughts, will also help.

However, we've no need to stop there, and a very effective way to gain more harmony within our mind is to 'lower the degree of difficulty', just as we did when we lowered the board in our earlier example.

Naturally, the easier it is, and more confident we are of completing any task, the more calm and harmonious we are likely to feel. This is a deep-down confidence from within, based on real things, as opposed to pumping ourselves up with false arrogance based on nothing.

'Lowering the degree of difficulty' is a term that I have used very loosely in this book, because there are simply so many different ways that we can achieve this. However, this is the principle of this whole book, and just how we make the task easier in order to create harmony within our mind and allow ourselves to be able to swing fluidly more often. You will be able to see the same basic theme throughout this book, as to how we can potentially improve and lower the degree of difficulty. Here are the areas where we can potentially look, that can help to give us a little more confidence by making the task a little easier.

Course management: Managing ourselves around the course sensibly, and in a way that best suits our own natural mentality and mindset. This isn't always choosing the easiest and safest option, and can sometimes mean that the more risky and difficult shot could be the one to choose, if it is the one that creates harmony within our mind. Yes, the easier, safer, more sensible shot is the one we would usually choose, but it can also happen that opting for the harder shot is the one that gives us the best chance of making a great swing, and makes the task easier, despite it appearing completely the opposite. This is the responsibility and skill of our conscious mind, to be as connected as possible to our subconscious, and learning to make the best decisions that keep us harmonious, while navigating ourselves sensibly around the course.

Improving our technique: This is where *Rtf* will differ the most to many of the more traditional ways of thinking, as we believe that good technique is very personal to each individual, and we would not teach preferences. However, finding the set of circumstances that suit us best, will clearly help to make the task much easier. This, we will try and cover more fully as the book progresses.

Equipment: Choosing the right club in any given situation and using equipment that we can comfortably manage and suits our present style of play.

That's it for now, but before we move on to the next chapter, this is a good moment to mention that while Mr Sensitive could be seen as a negative factor and the spoiler of so many good shots, *Rtf* coaching looks at it from a different perspective and therefore sees only the positive. Mr Sensitive may well be responsible for sabotaging the possibility of fluid, coordinated movement at times, however, he always has our best interests at heart and there may well be a very good reason for him acting in this way. Golf is a game with such tiny margins between success and failure, that a bad shot or outcome could happen at any time, even when we've managed to swing well: we've all missed with a perfectly well-struck putt, for example. Mr Sensitive is more highly tuned and aware of this than any other part of our mind, and when he senses danger, his first reaction will be to hold back free-flowing movement, just like applying the brakes in a car.

I've now realised that when Mr Sensitive is making it too hard for me to make the swings that I would like to, he probably has a very good reason. Therefore, this is my opportunity to learn something new about myself, and help Mr Sensitive to be able to trust once more.

Once again, you will begin to see a theme throughout this book. The more reasons you can give Mr Sensitive for staying calm, the greater your chances of success will be.

In short

Our goal is to create harmony in the mind, which can help us to swing with coordination and fluidity. One of the ways we can do this is to lower the degree of difficulty, and there are many sides from which we can actually achieve this.

ON THE FIFTH
THE SUBCONSCIOUS RESPONSE

*In which we consider the possibility that our swing is
nothing more than a subconscious response.*

This means that any golfswing, and all the different
positions within it, are a result of our own best
subconscious reaction to the set of circumstances that
have been presented by our conscious self.

Suddenly, we are looking at the golfswing from a
very different angle. Our golfswing and the positions
within it, are only an outer visual manifestation of the
workings that are going on much deeper within our
minds: of course, this and the shape, strength, and
flexibility of our body. If we change the workings
within, and anything that the conscious mind is
responsible for, then the subconscious reaction – our
golfswing – will automatically change too. I have now
witnessed this on many occasions, how people can
completely change their swing, without any need to
have even one single positional swing thought.

Bearing all this in mind, let's look at the factors that
are likely to go towards shaping or changing our swing.

If we can truly understand this, then we have a much better chance of being able to constructively improve our technique, in a way that is entirely based around ourselves as an individual, and genuinely serves to lower our degree of difficulty, as opposed to changing our swing mechanically to fit with an instructor's preferences. Here are some of the things that can be responsible for, or change, the positions in our swing.

Sabotaging the messages that go out to our smaller muscles

We need to mention this first, because it's not uncommon for us to block or hamper these messages, and when our swing suddenly loses coordination, the positions within it will be considerably different to the times when we have allowed ourselves to swing with fluidity. This is the main reason for our poor swings, and we should always be asking ourselves the question, 'Did we really swing as well as we had set out to?' If the answer is no, then we know exactly what has happened, and hopefully, at the end of this book, we may know which path to follow, in order to help this happen less frequently.

Our own personal stage of development

Yes, this is one area that so many friends wanting to help, or even golf instructors, often fail to take into account. A toddler will not throw a ball perfectly from day one, but soon learns without intervention. Of course, exactly the same thing applies to golf. Unfortunately, so often, we don't allow a person to develop naturally, just as he would with throwing, and we think that by teaching we can somehow help and speed up the process. Of course, by teaching someone as they develop, we are likely to be teaching them our own set of preferences. From this point onwards, we have no way of knowing just how difficult we might have made future development for them, as their own preferences are likely to be very different to our own. Allowing them to develop more naturally and being there as a mentor will be far more helpful for them. Not only this, but by forcing our pupil to think mechanically we will undermine the role of his Mr Computer, once again, disrupting the flow of messages going out to the smaller muscles.

Perhaps I could also add here, that many sports are based around some type of throwing action. If someone has played a lot of other sports, and then takes up golf, his muscles will be relatively well developed to swing a golfclub, and his own Mr Computer will already have built up some kind of program that understands the feeling of throwing. This will put this kind of pupil several steps ahead immediately.

Grip and stance

This could be either an accidental or deliberate change to either the pressure or the position of our grip. This will change the positions in our swing, for both mechanical reasons, and because our own subconscious reaction will have to be modified to adjust to this new set of circumstances in its attempts to still produce a good shot: which it will eventually have to do.

Any change to our ball position and posture will also change the response in our subconscious, and therefore the positions in our swing, for exactly the same reason.

Alignment

We may not always be aware of this, but our swing will always react to whatever direction our body happens to be pointing. Despite what many people may think, we never really lose complete contact with our target, once we have looked at it. In fact, we couldn't forget about it if we tried, and will always have an awareness of where it is. I've now stood behind thousands of golfers and can clearly see when a person has accidentally aligned himself in a way that does not marry well with the type of shot he is trying to hit. I've then watched how his subconscious mind has reacted and attempts to deal with this less-than-perfect scenario. And it is important to note here, that this is the big danger of learning to aim mechanically, as opposed to when our aiming is simply connected to the shot-picturing process.

This would be the equivalent of when you are trying to throw a ball at a target, and there is an ideal direction for your body to be pointing which subsequently makes it easy for your throwing arm to work freely and optimally. However, if your body is aiming in another direction altogether, you would still throw it towards the target, but it would become a lot more difficult and less efficient, lacking in both accuracy and power. This works exactly the same in golf, and so many of our bad shots happen this way. We mostly then later blame our swing, when in actual fact it has merely done its best under the difficult set of circumstances it has been lumbered with.

Shot picturing

I know many people think that they either don't do this, or they are not capable of it. However, I believe this to be untrue, and we all do it, only at different levels of capability, and even if we're unaware of it. Even as a novice, we look at where we want to go, and this in itself is a rudimentary start of shot picturing. Just the desire to hit the ball forwards towards a target, will have a major influence on the positions in our swing, which everyone will interpret in their own unique way. If the goal was simply to hit the ball, we all would probably pick the club up directly over our heads and hit straight down on top of it. Do you see what I mean?

Of course, more advanced shot picturing will have even more obvious effects on the way we swing and the positions within it. Imagine the differences from when you are trying to hit the ball low, high, draw, fade, straight, three quarter shot, or whatever.

We need to ask ourselves the same question in golf as we could easily do in other sports where the ball is not stationary. 'Which is it that comes first, is it the type of shot that we have decided to hit that decides the positions in our swing, or is it ourselves mechanically placing the club into positions that produces the desired shot?'

Our observations

We are all natural copiers; we simply can't help it. From the moment that we begin to play golf, we are looking at all the golfers around us, particularly the good ones. Depending on who we admire and are looking at, this will likely have some influence on the way we swing. That is until we learn to look more into ourselves, and worry less what others are doing. We can always learn some things from watching others, but the quicker we can tune into our own needs and feelings, the better are our chances of moving forward.

Our culture and upbringing

Yes, even this will have a significant effect on the positions and effectiveness of our swing, and perhaps more so than we'd imagine. If we are from a culture where we have been brought up to work all problems out scientifically, mathematically, and very seriously, our swing will likely evolve that way, looking potentially more stiff and mechanical. However, if we are from a more flamboyant and relaxed culture, our swing will evolve this way, and become more relaxed and flamboyant. If we then understand how our only basic is to free flow and whip the club through impact without any manipulation, we can clearly see how a more flamboyant culture may even produce a more effective golfswing. This wouldn't necessarily produce a better scorer, but potentially a better ball striker.

Injuries, our build, and body make-up

This needs little explanation, as I'm sure everyone understands how our own individual shape and flexibility will naturally produce a different swing. Of course, any kind of serious injury is likely to hamper our movement, and force us to form a new subconscious reaction in order to hit the ball as we would like.

It's worth noting here that within *Rtf* coaching, we don't recognise any preference of the way we are supposed to swing. We understand that our subconscious mind is doing its best to produce the required result, with whatever circumstances it is presented, just as long as we understand our one and only basic. For this reason, we have no reason to treat an injured, or physically handicapped golfer any differently.

Our own individual tendencies

Hopefully this is not difficult to see either. Some people may have a tendency to slice and some may hook, some too low and some too high. Once again, this will have a significant effect in the way their swing is likely to develop. It wouldn't be difficult to assume that Lee Trevino, Jim Furyk, Bubba, Couples, and many more, had a hook problem when they were younger, which has definitely influenced how they swing and play today.

Environment and lie

Yes, unfortunately we don't always play golf on a perfect and flat lie with no wind, and any change away from these ideal circumstances will create an unconscious reaction within our subconscious mind, trying to adapt to our new environment and still hit a good shot. We are rarely aware of these changes, just as we are not aware of small changes in our walking on different surfaces.

Equipment

This may not be quite so obvious, but should definitely not be ignored, as this can also be part of the jigsaw we are looking at. For example, if someone is using a driver that has too little loft to cope with their own natural clubhead speed and angle of attack, their subconscious will automatically take evasive action and still try to hit a good shot, despite the physical laws working against it. We have all seen this so often amongst amateur golfers, as they appear to have a completely different swing with their driver compared to their other clubs, and yet they are actually trying to do the same thing.

This scenario could equally apply to all types of shots, including the wedges and putter; in fact every club in the bag, for all kinds of different reasons.

What can we learn from this?

Players like Bubba, Furyk, Trevino, Darcy, even Nicklaus and many more had to believe that they could do better using their own instinctive approach than they would have, had they gone wholly with the teaching methods of the day. This would have taken an almost superhuman self-belief, and is perhaps the reason there are fewer players in this category; but this doesn't mean it's the wrong approach, simply that very few people are naturally mentally equipped to undertake this path. In fact their approach is very *Rtf*, in the sense that they play 'their' way; they do it their way. They have taken their own unique and individually specific approach to golf.

It's worth noting that we know for sure that these players are playing their own way, and instinctively, but I believe that all good players are playing more instinctively than even they know. It may not be so obvious, as the outward appearance of their swing and stance appears to fit more closely into what we would consider 'normal' or textbook, whatever that is.

In short

If we want to play as close to our maximum potential as possible, it's our job to find the set of circumstances that work most efficiently for ourselves, helping us to have the best possible opportunity to swing with complete fluidity and freedom.

PART THREE

ON THE SIXTH
ESTABLISHING OUR STARTING
POINT

In which we attempt to establish a platform from which we can make our first step towards real and sustained improvement.

Actually, there are two parts to this. The first part is our physical starting point where we try to connect with our best possible swing and subconscious response, at our present level of ability. Only then are we ready to move on and find further improvement.

The second part is to take an honest look at our present capabilities, and establish where we are in our head, with regards to our current capabilities. In this way we establish a personal datum against which it is easy to recognise new skills and improvement as it comes.

Establishing our physical starting point

The first thing we do, is to decide the type of shot we'll use to establish our starting point. It could be a putt, a chip, a full swing, or any type of shot we like. Let's assume in this instance we are going to find our starting point for a full swing, from a relatively flat lie with no adverse conditions, using the swing and type of shot that we would presently consider as our normal everyday swing. However, this is only for this particular example; eventually we will be able to see that we can repeat the same process for any type of shot we choose.

Likewise, we can choose any one of our clubs, but ideally we would choose the one we find the easiest to strike well, whichever one that might be. Many people would probably choose a 7 iron, or the like, but it really doesn't matter. However, for now at least, it would be best to stay with the club that we are most comfortable with.

The other key to this exercise is for us not to aim at any specific target. In fact, try to aim into absolutely nowhere and away from any target. This is because we don't want any reference, such as a target, to spoil our judgement. Now we're going to try and picture ourselves hitting the most perfect shot that we could possibly imagine. It must be one that is easily within our capabilities, and one that we have managed before. We may all have different ideas on how we judge what a great shot is, but that is not so important, and we can judge it as we see fit. What is important is that the shot feels just about as good as we can presently manage.

Most of us would probably judge a good shot by

the quality of the strike, the freedom of movement, and that overall feeling of making a good swing. In other words, one that is balanced, coordinated, with fluid movement and a good strike. The important thing to remember here, is that we are the sole judge of what is a good shot, and no one else. It has to feel good for us, and correspond to whatever our own present standard is. Even if it's a bit of a slice or a hook, if that's our present standard, and it feels like the best we can do, then we give it a mark of ten; it's entirely our own judgment. In other words, a shot that we are pleased with at our present level, and not one that say, Rory McIlroy might be satisfied with.

Okay, now we're going to have a go at hitting that shot, ideally, with no technical swing thoughts in our head. We're going to try to keep it as nothing more than a great feeling throughout the whole swing, from start to finish.

Next, we are going to give ourselves a mark out of ten, depending on how close we come to achieving that great feeling of our best shot. Obviously, we give ourselves a mark of ten if we've managed to produce a shot exactly as we had imagined. However, on each shot, we will give ourselves a mark out of ten as a reference to just how close we came to achieving that perfect shot. Now we simply keep going and see how close we can get to a ten, or the highest mark that we can possibly achieve. In the beginning, whatever results we are achieving, we'll try to stay clear of any mechanical thoughts. In other words, if we fail, we don't try to correct anything mechanically, and continue trying to capture 'that feeling'.

Okay, unless someone is actually a robot and not a

human being, it's probably safe to assume that our marks were somewhat varied? If they were, this is perfectly normal, and we will hopefully be able to clarify this in a moment. But first, we are hoping that we have been able to score a ten, or something very close to it. Hopefully, we can still remember that feeling now. Even if we can't, we would presumably recognise it as soon as we managed another one.

Right, let's assume that we have now managed a very high score, or preferably a ten. This is our opportunity where we can learn so many different things, so let's have a look at what they could be.

Firstly, we have actually established our starting point. Yes, we can now clearly see exactly what we are capable of, just as long as we can find the right situation that will help us to make that fluid and coordinated swing which gives us that great strike. This is probably a good moment to accept that golf is a sport and a competition against ourselves and other people, and it is up to ourselves to take care of the movement and the strike. In other words, it's up to us to follow up and complete something that we are already capable of doing.

This means that the more tens, or close to, we can make, the better player we are going to become. After all, we wouldn't expect in any other sport, to be able to make a wild uncoordinated slash at the ball and for it to drop in the spot exactly as we'd planned, with a perfect strike, now would we? Can you imagine doing that at say, tennis, and then asking what we had done wrong? Instead of focusing on what we did wrong, we can now shift our attention towards finding ways to make it easier for us to find that lovely, fluid and coordinated movement that we are already perfectly capable of. Reasonable?

Secondly, the exercise that we've just completed, is the equivalent of walking along the two-foot wide plank while it's still on the ground, as we've made the conditions as easy as possible. We can easily do it, just as long as we are in the right frame of mind and we haven't created a situation to make it harder. When we begin to aim at a target or play on the course, the consequences of failure become a little more serious. This would be the direct equivalent of beginning to raise our plank up into the air. In some cases, this could sharpen our focus and improve our walking, while others will start to wobble early on. The higher we go, the harder it becomes, and eventually there's a point when we're all finding fluid movement impossible, and are all clutching on with the whites of our knuckles showing. Of course, there are so many factors that will decide the height where each person will start to struggle with coordination, and we shall try to cover this as much as we can in this book. The better our understanding is of this, the easier it is to find improvement.

Thirdly, we can now see how we are perfectly capable of achieving a great strike without any swing thought; the subconscious was perfectly capable of taking care of the whole thing! Perhaps we didn't need to consciously control the swing with lots of swing thoughts as we have previously been led to believe.

Fourthly, we have now managed to achieve a feeling of what we are at least trying to do, on every full shot that we hit. It's not guaranteed, but it is likely, that the more ten swings that we are able to achieve, the lower we are able to score.

If we change clubs, the feeling is very similar. It might be a little more difficult on some of our other clubs, but at least we have now established what it is that we are trying to achieve. Preferably, we try not to use any descriptive words regarding our swing, and just keep it as our own personal feeling of a good swing and strike. We won't forget it, and we will always recognise it again when it turns up next. Words will only confuse the matter and can lead to us losing a clear picture of that special feeling. For example, some people may perceive a coordinated movement as being a slow one, as it both feels and looks like they have swung too quickly when they hit a bad shot. However, this is a misconception, as it is Mr Sensitive causing tension, and the lack of fluid, coordinated movement that has made the swing both feel and look too quick. If we were to focus on being slow, it is likely that our swing will eventually become too slow, which will almost certainly make it much harder to coordinate and swing with any kind of freedom or fluidity. An overly slow swing will probably create a lot of unwanted tension and rigidity.

Actually, adding to the above, words are, once again, our attempts to take control of the swing consciously, which is how we are presently taught and is deep within our learning culture. It would be just great if we could manage to break away from this pattern of thinking, and learn to really connect to, and accept, our own personal feelings, and keep them that way, as just that: our own personal feelings. We can never measure or create any kind of statistics based around our feelings, but learning to trust them only makes perfect logical sense. Why would we ever want to ignore them, while trusting someone else's judgment who can only see the visual exterior of all of the workings, and knows nothing of what's going on below the visible surface?

Lastly, we saw how our marks out of ten would have fluctuated considerably, for no particular reason. We can learn certain things from this. Firstly, this gives us our first opportunity to see how the balance within our mind can affect our ability to coordinate well, and how the positions in our swing might change, even though we are not trying to do anything differently.

We can also realise just how tight the margins are in golf, and it doesn't take much for us to mess up. This might sound negative to some people, but awareness is the key to being able to solve any problem. Neither does it hurt to be realistic and hence become a little easier on ourselves when we don't manage to do as well as we'd sometimes like. It's perfectly natural to fear the bad shot at golf, because of these tight margins, so it's no wonder that we struggle to coordinate at times, as we create an imbalance in the mind through doubting ourselves.

It's worth noting here how some players' marks out of ten will be fluctuating more than others. This will be either due to the type of personality they are, or just how damaging their bad shots actually are. If they are the fearless, bravado type, then this will translate over to Mr Sensitive, and he won't be as protective and cautious as he might otherwise have been, hence their swing may feel free-flowing and coordinated, even with a few bad shots. Conversely, if they are more of the cautious type or are 'over-trying', they may feel more tension in their swing. Both ways have their advantages and disadvantages, so neither way is either right or wrong, and both can be later worked on to find the best balance for playing well. Likewise, if their bad shots are particularly destructive, Mr Sensitive may be more on edge, and hence this could be another reason why a swing may feel inhibited or tense.

Once we've tried this on the range, some of you might want to try this out on the course, as this can really help in many ways. We simply take a scorecard out, and give ourself a mark out of ten for every single shot that we hit. Even if it's a six-inch putt, we still mark it. This is a great habit to get into, and is superb for making the transition away from mechanical thinking and beginning to rely on the amazing capabilities of our subconscious. We can also begin to see more clearly, the connection between a good feeling, strike, movement, and a great shot.

Establishing our mental starting point

This is all about having a realistic picture of the level that we are presently at, in each individual part of our game. If we are able to establish just how good we presently are, then we will clearly recognise any kind of improvement. The important thing here, is that we can start the ball rolling, and then keep the momentum going, experiencing small steps of improvement all the time.

I use the word realistic, because if we view our present ability too highly, it will be easy for us to become disappointed if we see ourselves not making those first initial important steps of improvement. So often, we make the mistake of viewing ourselves too highly, and then trying to take too big a step and become perfect, all in one go.

Some people may consider it to be negative to be so brutally honest with yourself, if you really are genuinely poor at some part of your game. However, here we are accumulating all the tools to be able to plot our way forwards, improving all of the time, so recognising where you are now is an important part of the process and is not negative in any way. In fact, quite the opposite!

If you were once good at something, but are now bad at it, forget about the past completely and try to accept your present position. Please keep remembering, that if we can stay true to this way of thinking, there is no reason why it shouldn't be forwards all the way to the eventual success we had always hoped for: and sometimes even more, as we surprise ourselves how good we can become.

In short

Establishing both our physical and mental starting point is a very important part of the process. Our early chapters are there to help us gain a better understanding of how we work and our subconscious mind. The following chapters are about giving us the tools that will make it impossible for us to ever become worse, and with a bit of patience and perseverance, there is no reason why improvement shouldn't become both inevitable and unlimited.

ON THE SEVENTH
PRACTICE AND PROGRAMS

In which we consider how we might further develop our subconscious mind to be able to perform at a higher level, with more intricate and accurate capabilities. This we can do by introducing some new ideas regarding the way we practice. These new ideas will also give us the opportunity to be able to connect more closely to our subconscious, and to develop the set of circumstances, where we can move closer towards realizing our full potential.

This is a key chapter, and not solely about a way to practice. It concerns the way we think when we play golf, so don't be put off if you're not a keen practicer.

I have seen this working now for the past four or five years, and can now confidently claim its effectiveness.

Before we talk about practicing, let's just look at how this way of thinking came about.

It's certainly no secret, that all the top players hit the ball extremely straight, and with great control.

Not only this, but when they're in trouble and have to hit a very imaginative recovery shot, they appear to be just as accurate, with no loss of control. Even when the wind is particularly strong and they are really having to shape the ball, and made to adapt their swing to each different unique situation; once again, they are still able to play with great accuracy and that same degree of control.

In these kind of scenarios, these players play more instinctively, as positional thoughts become nearly impossible, and they are literally forced to rely more heavily on the ability of their subconscious mind. Their conscious mind could not even attempt to cope with all the different sets of intricate and highly complex adjustments required for each individual shot and swing.

On the other hand, when any of us try to hit the ball perfectly straight, with a full swing, from a nice flat lie, and no wind; we all tend to revert to a more robotic, mechanical and 'conscious' way of thinking, as we try to repeat the same swing, over and over again.

For those of you that are not so used to playing so imaginatively, you could probably imagine the same thing regarding putting. When we are faced with a dead straight putt, our thinking generally becomes more mechanical. On the other hand, when the greens are fast and slopey, we tend to become less mechanical, and more instinctive and 'feely,' as we are now forced to calculate a complex equation between line and pace, which is, once again, too difficult for our conscious mind.

We now know that the more mechanical, positional and consciously aware we are, the less chance we have of gaining fluid movement. Likewise, the more instinctive and subconscious we are, the better are our chances of moving and swinging freely with great coordination.

In other words, the more consciously aware and mechanical we are, the more we tend to disrupt a perfectly functioning subconscious mind.

Bearing all this in mind, we really should ask the question as to how all the top players have learned to hit the ball so 'seemingly' straight and with such great control? Could it be possible that for the vast majority of their progression in golf, they weren't even aware of, or understood how they were developing, as it all happened deep within their own subconscious mind, just as they did when they learned to walk, throw a ball, and so on?

We all know that the top players have all got their own individual set of preferences, which they generally attribute as the 'whole' reason behind their straight hitting; even though these are constantly changing and variable. Given this, it's not difficult to see, that the considerably larger reason behind it all, clearly lies deep within their subconscious mind and nothing that they are even aware of.

At this point we could probably learn something from the late, great Seve Ballesteros.

Learning from Seve

Seve used to play instinctively, with incredible imagination and shot making ability, and far greater control than he was ever given credit for, especially in the beginning. You don't become number one player in the world without a real ability to control the ball. He sometimes looked a little wild, but a large part of this was due to his explosive power and the incredible distances he was able to hit the ball. His body was moving so fast and athletically at times, it would have been very difficult for him to always be able to maintain such perfect timing.

It's worth noting at this point: Seve was invariably wild when he was trying to hit the ball 'straight,' and was mostly pinpoint accurate when attempting a seemingly impossible and very imaginative shot, whilst trying to escape from trouble.

Seve was like a Formula One car whose engine had been tuned too highly, and was suddenly very difficult just to keep on the track. A hair trigger too hard on the accelerator, and the car is off the track. This would have been very different to say Nick Faldo, who was more of the 'easy to drive' and dependable type of car. Tragically, the second that Seve began to think more mechanically, and make his swing more 'one dimensional' and positional in an attempt to gain control and become more like Faldo, the absolute opposite happened. He completely lost both control and distance, in as dramatic a way as has ever been seen. His magical powers were gone, and he was left with absolutely no game at all: literally. As we know, most people blamed Seve's back problems, but I am far less convinced. I've seen many people with serious back issues, still hold on to an ability to strike the ball really well. I used to watch the way he was working on his game, and it looked more like an accident waiting to happen. I believe that the seed had been planted early on in his career, and this eventually grew into something that led to his eventual complete collapse. Not only that, he was far from the only player to suffer in this way, which includes all those with perfectly healthy backs!

The minute that Seve tried to hit the ball straighter, he took his first initial steps away from playing subconsciously, and began to become more mechanical and consciously aware of his swing. It's a bit late now, but Seve probably needed to do the polar opposite of the advice he received, and what he thought was the best thing to do. He actually needed to connect 'even more so' with the powers of his subconscious mind, especially because of his extreme 'formula one car' like characteristics. The more control he tried to gain, the more he lost. Hence the expression, 'sometimes you have to lose control to gain control.'

Of course, Faldo was not faced with the same kind of problem as Seve, and probably appeared to hit the ball straight, and swing rather mechanically. In fact, all of his success was acclaimed to the positional changes he appeared to make to his swing. However, appearances don't always tell the full, or even the true story. I can once remember Faldo severely reprimanding a fellow pro for simply asking him if he was trying to hit the ball straight. He glared at the other pro and said, 'Why would anyone ever want to try and hit the ball straight!!?' Yes, Nick played far more instinctively than we ever give him credit for - and that some people would have us believe - and probably a lot more so than he even thinks himself.

So, what have we learned so far?

Hopefully we are beginning to see a pattern. 'Straight, square and repetitive' will tend to encourage us to be more consciously aware and mechanically minded, which can consequently put a spanner in the workings of our subconscious mind, making fluid, coordinated movement difficult.

At this point, it could be worth noting, that tennis and table tennis players hit the ball with slice and topspin, and never stand square and hit the ball 'straight,' and they certainly don't appear to have a problem with accuracy. And likewise for Ten-pin bowlers, who also never bowl completely straight, arguably for exactly this reason.

Okay, now we should be ready to put this knowledge to work, find our recipe for success, and look at a way we can practice.

Practicing

To begin with, I'd like you to try this simple exercise.

First pick a target, and then aim to a point that is around 10 - 20 degrees to the left of your chosen target. Once you've set up and aimed at this 'new target,' simply try to hit a shot towards your original target. Hit a few shots like this, and then do exactly the same thing, but this time aiming to the right of your target.

This is great practice, and a very good start to learning how to become more subconscious, as it is impossible to do this exercise while thinking positionally and mechanically.

Most 'right handers' will usually find it easier when aiming a little left, but it isn't unusual for a person to prefer to aim to the right, as the great Bobby Locke once showed us with incredible success.

You can do this exercise with any club from a driver right down to a putter. The important thing here is that this is our first steps to move away from mechanical and robotic ways of thinking, that have arguably originated from trying to hit the ball straight, while trying to stand perfectly square.

Hopefully you noticed how good you actually were, even though you weren't actually standing square? Also, how good our subconscious is at finding the target anyway, and a good shot is certainly not dependant on a perfectly square stance, and not necessarily easier either. If you don't find this easy, as some people might not, continue with the exercise intermittently, and you'll soon get the hang of it.

Okay, this was our first exercise when practicing, and this might be more than enough for some people, and helping them to become less mechanical in their thinking. But for those that are a little more ambitious, we can now move on and learn how to further develop our subconscious by practicing more imaginatively.

Before we start, we should be aware that for many people this might be a step too far, and 'just to make contact' might be as imaginative as they would want to get. We should also know that this is not meant as a quick swing fix. This is all about taking our first steps down a pathway where we are both programming and learning more subconsciously, together with eventually opening up new possibilities to tap into so much more of Mr Computer's full capabilities.

Also, this will require a certain amount of trial and error as we practice, and this will be our best opportunity to begin to learn so much more about ourselves. Here we begin to find our own best set of circumstances that help to keep Mr Sensitive calm.

So, bearing everything in mind, we could start by becoming more creative when we practice, trying to hit the ball with different shapes: draw, fade, high, low, or any one combination of these. As you become proficient at this, it would be worth noting which combination or type of shot you are best at, as this could later be very useful out on the course.

We could probably start by just learning to draw and fade, and then introduce high and low later. This is not meant as just an exercise, and the sheer act of doing is no guarantee that we'll improve. The goal is to become as proficient as we possibly can, and learn how to execute them with some real control.

Don't forget, we're all individuals, and there is no wrong or right way to do things. If we were to look at a group of top players, they would all be thinking and doing things differently, so why should we be any different? The key is to remember that there are no rules as to the way we stand or aim; we can stand in any direction that feels comfortable, and can use any grip, clubface angle or stance that helps to produce the type of shot we're trying to hit.

So, this is going to require a little bit of personal effort and application. However we can help a little, without making the mistake of giving you a set of rules that you must follow. *This is all about finding a set of rules that are specifically designed around you!*

A little help

It's best to picture a draw starting out to the right and drawing back to the target, or even finishing just a fraction to the right of our target. A draw that starts to the right, or even straight, and crosses over to finish to the left of our target is mostly an ineffective shot, and of little use to us. Also, by picturing it this way, it will give the right kind of signals to our subconscious mind, which will begin to lead to the right kind of swing.

This same principle applies, but vice versa for the fade.

Now, all we have to do is to find our own ideal set of circumstances that make it even easier for us to hit a draw and fade with real control. This is any combination of grip, clubface angle, way to aim, stance and way to picture that gives us the most confidence and ability to hit these shots, which is entirely governed and decided by our own individuality.

For both shots, I would probably recommend that a good part of your focus is on where you want the ball to start, and imagine yourself swinging the clubhead approximately down that line, or ideally even a little more left or right. I may not be a big fan of technical gadgets, but this is an area where a launch monitor can be used to give helpful feedback and speed up the learning process. However, a reasonable knowledge of ball flight laws and watching the ball, can work equally as well for those that don't have this possibility.

If you can start the ball out in the right direction, you've got 50% of it right, and that's pretty good to begin with, and could be your initial goal. Then simply stand in a way that would make it comfortable for you to both swing and start the ball in the direction you have pictured.

Above everything, just to understand the type of spin that we're putting on the ball should be the best help of all to start our journey of practicing this way.

How do we now hit the ball 'straight?'

A straight shot is now simply something that is in-between a fade and a draw. We can drop all the complicated set of positional instructions and analysis that come together with learning to hit the ball straight. There is no need to learn and practice all of the exact and 'correct' positions that we once thought were an essential part of playing good golf. It's so much easier when we have learned something that is 'a little bit over' and 'a little bit under,' and then we're just trying to capture the feeling of something that's somewhere in-between the two, which may not even be 'square' anyway.

This way, we are learning to play golf subconsciously, and there is no need to fall into the trap that comes with overly conscious and mechanical thinking.

There's no need to actually practice hitting the ball straight either, because this way we are liable to slip back into thinking more mechanically once again.

Rather think of it as, the better we can become at hitting the ball with draw and fade under control, the better we will automatically become at hitting the ball straight.

Actually, from all we've learned so far, there could even be a question whether we should even try to hit the ball straight at all, at least from a square stance?

Many of the top players will feel some kind of bias, one way or the other, even when they are trying to hit the ball straight; or at least what they might interpret as straight.

I can remember when Ian Woosnam was trying to hit the ball 'straight,' he actually felt like he was hitting a low fade! Only recently, I heard Henrik Stenson say more or less the same thing. Actually, the present trend of much of the 'method' mechanical coaching on The Tour, is actually suggesting a fade bias, although this is both expressed and learned as positions which they have to try and achieve, as opposed to learning more instinctively.

Hopefully, considering everything, this will at least encourage many of you to practice this way. Then as soon as you feel ready, slowly begin to introduce it onto the course.

It's likely that you'll find one particular combination of these shots easier than the others. Naturally, when you're playing, it's probably best to choose whatever it is that comes easiest. The ultimate goal is to be equally comfortable with all types of shots, and be able to choose whichever shot suits any particular set of circumstances. However, don't be discouraged if you're not able to entirely achieve this, as very few players can ever lay claim to this luxury; becoming good at just one of them works just fine too. However, continue to practice with imagination and all of the shots.

Practicing this way is not only helping us to become more instinctive, but it is also helping us to learn more about ourselves. For example; I generally picture the ball going fairly high, as I've found out that I can easily lose control when I try to hit the ball too low. However, some of my pupils have done the complete opposite; it's all about finding the formula that works best for you.

"Fades and draws are not something that should be exclusive to only the top players, while the rest of the world continue to struggle, trying to hit a shot that is arguably the hardest one of all of them! And especially from a perfectly square stance!

Can we forget all technique this way?

I don't want to give the impression that this book is solely about the mind, and that technique is now irrelevant. However, we have learned the dangers of mechanical thinking.

I prefer to think of it as we are learning to find the right set of circumstances that suit our own Mr Sensitive, while trying to remain as instinctive as we possibly can.

This will include all of the things that our conscious mind is responsible for, and that certainly is not the swing itself! Just to remind us, this is the grip, grip pressure, the stance, shot picturing, decision making and equipment. We should probably add the dialogue within our mind too.

In short

Imaginative practicing and thinking will encourage us to be more connected to the subconscious mind whilst also helping to build the programs within it. At the same time, we are using our own bit of trial and error to help us to find the most effective combination of grip, clubface angle, stance and shot picturing that works best for us as an individual.

We now know, that the more mechanical and positionally aware we become, the less subconscious we generally are, blocking the messages going to the smaller muscles, and making fluid coordinated movement very difficult. We are now beginning to see how trying to be 'straight' and 'square' can lead us towards more conscious and mechanical ways of thinking.

N B. In this book, we often talk about the things that the conscious mind is responsible for, one of which is 'shot picturing.' I feel that it should be mentioned that this is very similar to when you picture, or decide to hit, a shot at tennis, throw paper in the basket, bowl a cricket ball, or any other kind of physical action. You first decide what you want to do, and then you can also vaguely see yourself doing it and completing the task. If you were going to hit a topspin at tennis, you can actually picture the kind of action that is required. It's not frame by frame or positional, but it is a vague overall picture of how your body will feel and even how it probably looks as it completes the task successfully. If we refer this over to golf, you could actually say that this is some kind of swing thought, which, in a way it is. However, we don't want to make this positional, mechanical or at the forefront of our thoughts. Rather keep it just as vague as you would in any other physical motion that you do, and allow the subconscious mind to take full control and to do its job.

ON THE EIGHTH
GETTING DOWN AND RELAXED

In which we look a little closer at the Rtf basics and how this may be able to help the developing golfer.

So, moving on. Can we remind ourselves how every shot we are faced with is played with a certain level of fear of a bad shot? No matter how confident we might feel, there is always an underlying fear of missing due to the incredibly small margins in golf. Sometimes this fear comes to the surface, as we play the shot, and sometimes it doesn't. Once again, this may sound negative to many people, but it really isn't, because we are trying to use this awareness to help us to problem solve, and work in our favour. Okay, let's take a look at what happens when that fear comes to the surface, and the chain of events that follows.

Firstly: The process obviously starts in our head and creates an imbalance in the mind as we begin to express fear or doubt.

Secondly: This fear or doubt often then translates to a facial expression of tension.

Thirdly: This tension is also felt throughout our body.

Obviously, the source of the problem starts within the mind, but here we're going to look at the resulting tension in our bodies. I'd like you to try a little test for me. Try to imagine that you've seen a ghost, and actually do the wide-eyed expression of shock on your face, how you would imagine you'd look if you saw one. As you do it, try to be aware of your body and how it feels. Did it tense up? Was there any part of your body that felt like it involuntarily lifted upwards? Was it your shoulders? Could you feel how the tension started in your shoulders and forced them to come up? This seems to be universal, but where the tension travels after that is more random and personal to each individual. This knowledge can potentially help us a little.

If we are hitting a shot, and suddenly our fear of missing becomes predominant, the expression on our face will change, and our shoulders will tense, and lift involuntarily! All of this occurs at some stage before impact, usually as we are swinging down towards the ball. It may not be the same expression as if you saw a ghost, but it would certainly look strained and tense. Then, the feeling in your body would be like everything has involuntarily lifted upwards, and in particular your shoulders. Can you picture yourself, or even someone else doing this?

This is likely to be where the expression 'you lifted your head' originated from. Yes, it wasn't our head after all, it was our shoulders, and it all started in our mind as we began to experience our fear and lack of trust.

Can you imagine yourself coming into the ball with shoulders that are up and tense? If you can, could you also imagine the clubhead to be swishing through impact freely, at the same time? No? Can you feel how it simply couldn't happen? It's almost like putting the brakes on the clubhead, and it just won't swing through freely, no matter how hard you try. Or put another way, you lose the feeling of the weight of the clubhead.

Ideally, for the long-term benefit, it's the mental process we would like to help most. However, understanding the process also gives us an opportunity where our conscious mind can potentially help the subconscious, by programming it with some new information. In other words, an opportunity to develop a new 'feel'. Okay, so what can we do about it?

Firstly, we already know that we could help the process by lowering the degree of difficulty, and helping to improve the dialogue in our mind.

Secondly, we could learn to relax our facial muscles. This is a widely used tip, and one that can be reasonably effective. If you watch Lee Westwood, he plays with his mouth open, and this really helps to keep the face relaxed. You'll probably notice how it's actually quite difficult to tense your body whilst keeping your face relaxed. This exercise can work, but the danger is when this becomes a primary swingthought and we are overly focused on doing it. If it moves away from being just a soft or background swingthought, it could then become counterproductive.

And thirdly, we could try the exercise which I personally prefer. Yes, this is my preference, nothing more than that.

For this, we go back to the exercise we did while establishing a starting point. Only this time we are going to add an extra layer. Remember how we didn't aim at anything in particular, and tried to make our best 'ten swing'? A swing that felt as coordinated and balanced as we could possibly manage at our present level of playing?

Okay, this time I'd like you to do this again, only this time to hold the follow through position for a few seconds. Then, as you are standing there, just become more bodily aware and try to feel how relaxed and down your shoulders are. If they feel like they are up and tense, then try to relax them, allowing them to drop with no tension at all. Did you feel how your balance improved? Now, you are beginning to connect with this feeling of swinging through with relaxed shoulders.

Once again, try not to turn this into a hard and fast swingthought, you won't forget it anyway once you've connected with it. Now try another swing, and once again hold your finish position and feel how down and relaxed your shoulders are. Don't forget that this is a soft swingthought, and your focus remains on producing your best ten swing. Simply make a note as to how down and relaxed your shoulders are. This is not a position that you 'have to' achieve, simply a checkpoint as to how relaxed they were.

Hopefully, once you've practiced this for a while, you'll begin to see the following chicken and egg equations forming. The more freely the club swishes through, the more down and relaxed the shoulders are, and the more balanced you subsequently feel. If the clubhead is not swishing fluidly through impact, your shoulders will be up and tense in the follow through, and your balance will be poor. If your shoulders are relaxed, the clubhead is likely to swish through more freely.

This is a great exercise to help create the feel for a free-flowing clubhead through impact. However, please don't make the mistake of turning it into a primary swingthought, as we would be making that same old mistake once again, and turning it into something that is mechanical, and forcing ourselves into a position.

This works very well for both the long and the short game. Very worthwhile giving this a go if you've suffered any chipping woes. It may not be guaranteed, but it will put you in good stead, as an initial step towards gaining back some success.

In my opinion, all golf tips should come with a warning. This is not meant as a tip which then becomes the centre of your focus. I've seen so many over emphasise the word 'relax', and if this person tries too hard, they run the risk of becoming sloppy. In fact, if any thought is overemphasised, it can create an unwanted over-awareness. However, this is a great exercise to create a feel of the clubhead free flowing through impact. Once you've captured this feel, you can't forget about it, even if you wanted to. So move on, don't think about it, and continue to play with instinct and feel.

In short

Relaxed shoulders will help you to capture the feel of a free-flowing swish through impact.

PART FOUR

ON THE NINTH
LEARNING THE ART OF TRIAL
AND ERROR

In which we investigate whether trial and error still has a place in our high-tech golf world. My feeling is that we may have just missed its true meaning and potential.

The concept of trial and error is hardly something new. However, it has now become something of a dying art, and has been slowly replaced by high technology, statistical analysis, and science, where the answers are more instant, and appear to be more concrete and clear-cut. This is now generally where we lay our faith, whilst in the meantime, instinct, intuition, and our own feelings, are pushed deeper and deeper into the background.

Trial and error, as we presently know it, could easily be ineffective if put in the wrong hands. However, let's see if we can manage to unveil its true potential.

The first step

We take the following words completely out of our golfing vocabulary. These are, 'wrong', 'right', 'correct', 'should', 'shouldn't', 'must', 'mustn't', and 'have to'. And when we say take them out, we really mean Take Them Out! Then, we're going to replace all these words with just two: 'better' or 'worse'.

Just think about it. There can't possibly be a correct way to do things when all of the top players stand differently, swing differently, and think differently. And probably the best question we could all ask ourselves is this: would the likes of Jim Furyk, Eamon Darcy, Bubba Watson, Fred Couples, Lee Trevino, Jack Nicklaus, Ben Hogan, and perhaps even most of the tour, have become great or even good players, if they had adhered wholly to doing things correctly, and had not listened and learned to understand themselves and their own feelings? How good do you think Jim Furyk would have become, if he had been able to copy everything that Rory McIlroy does? Subjective of course, but I suspect he may not have even been good, let alone great. None of these players, and probably even the majority of successful players, have been afraid to break free from the trend, and listen to their own feelings, whilst doing their own bit of trial and error.

Besides, what's right today is often wrong tomorrow, as golfing knowledge is certainly not static, and is never the finished article. Many people try to prove their point by quoting 'scientific facts', but these seemingly 'set in stone' facts are only valid within the boundaries of our present knowledge.

Often a new and previously undiscovered dimension is uncovered, and suddenly the science no longer adds up. So many of golf's so-called facts come in to this category, as they are not connected to a knowledge and understanding of how our mind is working. We know that our subconscious mind is the motor of the golfswing, and we also know that the balance within it is unstable and often unpredictable, making it impossible to measure in any way. Basically, as soon as you involve the human mind, it makes solutions very difficult to entirely nail down. Indeed, I can still remember when I decided to make up a rule of my own. This rule was, 'never make up a rule', because the minute you do, someone will come along and squash it completely.

So now we are left with these two words, 'better' or 'worse'. Clearly, we would never do anything that actually makes us worse, so now we can only either remain the same, or we can get better. Already this is a better starting point than previously, as so many people often manage to get worse while trying to get better. Previously, we may have persevered because we are told that something is 'correct', but now this idea has been removed, it would be madness to continue with something that was showing no positive results whatsoever. Of course, there are some things that may take a little time before they become a fully working program within our subconscious mind, but they would have to be showing lots of positivity immediately to even consider any thoughts of perseverance.

Dropping the word 'correct', forces us to focus more on ourselves and find our own way, as opposed to following a set of rules that have not been designed specifically around us. This doesn't mean that we ignore all ideas that appear to be preferences for some other players, but we have the mindset and confidence to firmly accept that we are on our own journey, which may be very different to anyone else's. Only sensible trial and error has the true answers.

The second step

As we begin our trial and error, we do the best we can to drop all of our own natural prejudices: we all have them, we simply can't help it. However, any answers we find as a result of a bit of trial and error will be distorted and not necessarily the truth, unless we are able to become aware of, and able to discard our prejudices.

If we have a natural prejudice against something, this will immediately start an imbalance within our subconscious mind. Mr Sensitive is likely to react and display signs of anxiety, generated by our bias, thus making fluid movement more difficult. Imagine if I asked someone to make a change to their stance that was a bit out of the normal, but I had a good reason to think that it might suit him or her. They then became increasingly irritated, as they struggled to coordinate their swing, while their stance felt really uncomfortable. This feeling of discomfort that we would likely experience, is nothing more than Mr Sensitive reacting, as he worries whether Mr Computer's program will work. The result is usually a stiff and awkward swing, together with lots of poor shots. However, if I then told this person that Rory McIlroy stands this way, his prejudice against it is likely to be reduced, and this may be the right kind of calming dialogue that will help to pacify Mr Sensitive, and help this person make an unbiased judgement as to whether the stance had any positive effect, and was indeed an improvement... or not?

The same situation might apply if I asked the vast majority of men to try a lady's or senior flex shaft. They'd probably swing very poorly as Mr Sensitive reacts to their negativity, and they'd be left with thinking that the flex was not suited to them, when in fact it may well have been. However, if I changed the label to stiff, and told them that it was the most popular shaft on Tour, the outcome would probably be very different, as Mr Sensitive would be so much calmer and more patient to find out the true and untainted answer.

In short, our goal is to always find out the true answer, and not one that has been distorted by our own natural prejudices. If we can become aware of our prejudices, then we will find it easier to push them into the background, giving ourselves a chance to find real answers. So, when trying something new, unless we have managed to make a fluid, coordinated, and non-manipulated swing, we can't possibly have learned anything.

The third step

Having rejected the word 'correct', there are no real boundaries within our possibilities for trial and error. This is potentially a good thing, but it could also become a bad thing, as it can be like a rudderless boat, with no real direction. This third step is to help us to find our own rudder.

First of all, we never undertake any trial and error exercise without a clear direction as to what we are trying to achieve. A sympathetic coach or mentor can be helpful here, and to keep us on the right path, give us expert feedback, and as a supplier of some fresh ideas. However, we must be careful they are not preaching their own preferences, while not understanding our individualism. Either way, with a coach or not, we are the ultimate judge of ourselves and our own feelings, and much of our trial and error can be done alone. If we do receive some advice or a tip, we are now ready to quickly discard it, if we don't feel like it is designed around ourselves and fits in with our present way of playing and thinking.

The key for any swingthought, if we feel the need to have one, is that it doesn't interfere with the incredible feats of the subconscious, and therefore allows it to do the things that we could never even begin to understand or even calculate. Ideally, any swingthought would be picturing the swing as a whole, from start to finish, whilst hitting the shot we have opted for. It would also be soft, as opposed to exact, detailed, and positional, and focused on one particular point during the swing. If we choose the latter here, we will have channelled the power of our subconscious into achieving this exact position, and away from hitting the shot that we had pictured. In other words, we will have obstructed so many of the messages going out to our smaller muscles, as Mr Sensitive is quick to sense the problem. By picturing the swing as a whole, whilst hitting the desired shot, we will keep our subconscious firmly focused on the real task at hand, which is to hit a great shot.

Just to make it clear, a soft focus is more vague, and is generally just a distant feeling, whereas a hard focus is more exact, positional, and focuses on one particular point of the swing. Eventually, there is probably no reason to have any conscious swingthought at all, as more and more is handed over to the subconscious; however, there will always remain a very distant feeling or picture of how we're planning to swing.

Ideally, our trial and error is only on the things that our conscious mind is responsible for. These things are our grip, stance, ball position, aim, shot picturing, and decision making. The final decision will always be down to the conscious mind during these processes, however, our subconscious is still very much present, even here. The more we can learn to leave to the subconscious, the smoother becomes the transition when the conscious mind hands the job over to Mr C.

The last step

While there's not much that feels worse than playing really badly, whether it's for a day, a couple of holes, or longer period of time, I would suggest that herein lies a great learning opportunity. We certainly don't learn a lot when everything is going our way; if anything at all. Anyone who has gone on to achieve remarkable things will always tell you about just how many mistakes they made along the way. It's virtually unheard of for someone to get an easy ride to achieving greatness. So, it's well worth remembering, that our bad periods are just the time for a good bit of sensible trial and error and a real opportunity to learn more about ourselves. Not only that, but the more we know about ourselves, the better we can potentially become. So try to view it as positive: and besides, we are now developing the tools where problem solving becomes so much easier.

Michael Jordan said, 'I've failed over and over and over again in my life and that is why I succeed.'

Finally

It might not be considered as sexy amongst today's scientific approaches, but when it comes to matters regarding the human mind, and its unstable nature, a certain amount of trial and error will be needed. We cannot measure or see the activity within our own mind, let alone that of somebody else's. Sensible trial and error, while focused on our own feelings, simply has to be part of our journey on our road to maximising our potential: the more we can learn about ourselves, the better we can potentially become.

ON THE TENTH
THE ONE SHOT THEORY

In which we put forward a concept which leads us towards sustainable improvement.

The One Shot Theory is a huge part of this book, and can be as effective as you want it to be. I've now seen this in operation for the past four or five years, and it has exceeded any previous expectations that I might have had. Golf is more fun when you can see permanent improvement, while having so many different options of how you can achieve it. However, The One Shot Theory is much more than that, and its real capabilities are less obvious. Things may be a little slower and improvement is gradual, but in time, people are capable of things that you would previously have considered impossible and out of reach.

Hopefully, we have now accepted that there cannot possibly be any real right or wrong in golf. If so, this means that we no longer need to make that giant leap that exists between the two, which so often ends in failure. We can also see the advantages of how we can use trial and error to develop further, whilst making the most of our own individualism and personal qualities. In this chapter, we are looking for the ideal mindset to help us make the most of these new circumstances we find ourselves in: this I refer to as the One Shot Theory.

So, we choose any area of our game, where we would like to see new improvement. It doesn't matter which part, and can be absolutely anything we like. We might first look where we feel our weaknesses lie, but this doesn't necessarily have to be the case. Our goal then becomes to find some kind of improvement that might add up to just one shot per round. It doesn't matter how we manage to achieve this, all it has to be is something that could amount to one shot per round. We are no longer governed by trying to do something correctly. This is now all about us, and finding something that helps us to become better, and is only focused around us as an individual. We may find the inspiration from someone else, but it still has to add up to a one-shot difference for us, and not influenced by another person's positive experience, only our own.

If our chosen course of action turns out to be two, three, or even half a shot or less, it doesn't matter, as any kind of improvement is worth having: we're getting better. If we manage to make enough of these kinds of changes, this will soon add up to something really significant: a lot better.

For example, if we average hitting six fairways per round, and we can find a way to hit seven, then we have potentially achieved our goal. It doesn't matter how we achieve this either. It could be the way we think, course management, a new driver, shot picturing, new grip, small change of stance, better temperament: it doesn't matter. Either way, we'll be getting to learn something new about ourselves. Get as creative as you like; it only has to be one more fairway, and doesn't have to be correct or perfect, or even where we are finally going to end up; just one shot!

This idea that once we get something right 'that's it', is not only a myth, but it is also an unhelpful way to think if we are going to realise our true potential. Our game will generally be a moving, growing thing, which changes all the time, and is never stationary and complete. Once we can accept this way of thinking, we begin to see how we may never run out of ideas as to how we can find improvement. So be ready to move on, when you see your next opportunity to improve further still.

If we can manage to be one shot better due to thinking this way, this is nothing to ignore. However, there are some enormous unseen benefits, which we should also be aware of.

Firstly, when we managed to discard the notion that there is a correct way to do things, we simultaneously opened up the boundaries of how and where we can find improvement. We are no longer governed by a set of rules that we'd assumed we had to adhere to. We can find improvement whenever, and from wherever, we like.

Secondly, we will soon find that the momentum has swung more in our favour, where finding improvement is predictable and relatively easy. We are always going to hit some highs and lows, but there is no reason why the trend shouldn't always be moving in the right direction. After all, we know that our bad periods are only an opportunity to learn something more about ourselves, that we wouldn't otherwise have had.

Thirdly, golf actually becomes more fun when there are so many ways and new opportunities to find improvement.

And lastly, we can create a situation where each small piece of improvement leads on to even more improvement. Yes, as we begin the upward trend, our confidence begins to grow which rather quickly leads on to a better dialogue within the mind, which results in a lot more relaxed and coordinated swings. We're into a virtuous circle as opposed to a vicious one, which most of us will have encountered as we learned our game.

Obviously, I've seen the One Shot Theory working and in action, and what has surprised me most, was how a person ended up being capable of things that previously would have seemed impossible. This seemed to be due to the fact that they didn't try to do it in one giant leap, and one day it just happened, and suddenly they could do it. Often, much to their surprise! They didn't have to go through any pain or have to take a step backwards; they were just suddenly able to achieve things that previously seemed unfeasible, and often looked beyond their capabilities.

In short

Improvement can come from absolutely anywhere! Any small piece of improvement is significant and should not be ignored. Nothing is permanent and fixed, and we will always find new ways to keep moving forward. So, don't look back and don't be afraid to just keep moving on: it produces golf growth of the very highest order.

PART FIVE

ON THE ELEVENTH
AGING GOLFERS

*In which we look at how our golf might be deteriorating
unnecessarily as we get older, and how we can potentially reverse
the downward trend.*

Have you experienced any of these symptoms as
you have gotten older?

- Loss of balance.

- Stiffer, shorter swing.

- Difficulty releasing the club freely through
impact, with a lack of power and speed.

The likelihood is that you have, at least to some
degree. Now we can't guarantee to miraculously cure
all of these, but we can probably do more than you
might imagine. I have now seen older golfers showing
vast improvement, and often getting longer, even at
the age of sixty-nine.

I should also mention that this has happened

despite these people being pretty stiff in normal life. None of them stretch or exercise other than playing golf, either. Perhaps, if we also added an exercise program, they would benefit further still?

So, first let's try to understand why we may have experienced these symptoms, which may not be entirely down to the physical deterioration of our bodies as we age.

I was once told that the deterioration in my balance was all down to a natural loss of core strength as you age, which seemed reasonable enough, but I now realise this had very little, or nothing to do with it. We often look for mechanical answers, but this is far from the complete picture, and there is so much more that we can learn in this area, as to why we may experience some of these aging problems throughout our game.

The first thing to notice is that you don't have to be especially flexible to swing a golfclub.

Try to make a full and relaxed practice swing and see just how fully you are able to swing. This is not a test where you have to achieve the industry's idea of what a full swing looks like, but more like how it was compared to when you were in your twenties and thirties. Some of you may struggle a little, but all of you are likely to be able to make a more relaxed and fuller swing than you'd imagine. Try not to restrict your movement in any way, allowing your arms to soften and your feet to move, and certainly don't become obsessed with keeping your head still! Better than you thought? At least compared to the one when you are actually hitting a shot?

So, why can't we swing as freely when we hit the ball?

This will vary from person to person, but we all tend to grow up with an ever rising sense of caution. Most of our caution naturally develops with age, and from experiencing some of the things in life that we have now seen can potentially go wrong. This works exactly the same in golf as it does in life. The more bad shots we witness and the more things that go wrong, the more cautious we are likely to feel. The Veteran Tour players are the ones that are the most vulnerable here, because they have all been playing for such a long time, and every shot still means, and has meant, so much to them. For this reason they are the ones that could potentially be carrying the most mental baggage.

Anyway, the caution we feel is our old friend Mr Sensitive, trying to protect us from impending danger. Once again we have the same scenario as when we imagined that we were walking on a plank which was forty storeys up in the air. Can you picture yourself, as the board gets higher and higher? You are no longer striding out confidently, and your footsteps are getting shorter and tighter as your caution and fear grows: 'shorter' and 'tighter' are the key words here. Suddenly, balance becomes more difficult and we stretch out our arms to use them to counterbalance, and now we are seeing how our balance can be affected. Yes, Mr Sensitive takes over and blocks the messages going to the smaller muscles. So, here we are once again: we need the smaller muscles to enable us to perform tasks that require balance and coordination, and now they are out of action, or performing well below par at best. It's not difficult to see how the same symptoms we experience as the board gets higher, work their way into our golfswing, and in particular as we grow older and are carrying a whole lifetime of mental baggage.

This is clearly what happened to Seve. His swing became shorter and tighter as he grew older. He began to hit the ball much shorter and much wider, as he struggled so desperately to be able to coordinate his swing. Unfortunately, Seve was pretty vulnerable to some poor advice, and he got more than his fair share of it, and it clearly wasn't compatible with his own personal golfing DNA. Eventually, his own Mr Sensitive completely lost trust and took over entirely, and no longer allowed any kind of freedom of movement.

So what can we do about it?

To begin with, the awareness of the problem and knowing what we're dealing with, is a great start towards success.

Just as it is for all golfers, our goal is to give Mr Sensitive as many reasons as we can as to why he should relax and allow Mr Computer a free rein once more. Of course, with younger golfers, Mr S will probably be more relaxed, as he may not have so many negative experiences stored in his subconscious. Whereas the older players may need to know themselves a little better, and have a few more good reasons as to why Mr S doesn't need to be full of doubt or concern.

This is where we use the One Shot rule to gradually chip away at helping Mr Sensitive. The more that Mr Sensitive relinquishes his stranglehold and hands back control to Mr Computer, the more relaxed, loose, and fluid our swing will feel.

Then we could try to recapture the more flamboyant side of our nature. Not to the point of recklessness of course, but there is no need to do this if we adopt a good strategy.

When we practice, we do it just as we described in the chapter on practicing, or even more so. Then, as we gain in competence, we begin to introduce this more and more into our game, out on the course. We are now really beginning to picture shots, and playing more instinctively and with a sense of adventure. The more instinctive you can become, the more 'in touch' you are with Mr Computer. Now we are really learning to exploit the full capabilities of our subconscious mind, and Mr Computer. The smaller muscles are now receiving the messages clearly, and our swing is becoming more fluid and coordinated, better balanced, and will begin to feel less restricted. Here we are really starting to reverse the effects of aging. Adventuresome and flamboyant are not traits we would normally put together with aging.

Then we could also try to let go of the mindset that, by controlling our swing, we will be improving our ability to hit the ball straight. Long and straight hitting comes from a free-flowing and coordinated swish through the ball, and not a tight, controlled, and mechanical action. Allowing our arms to soften and allowing yourself to move freely will only help us to regain our youthful feelings. Stay away from this thought process that less moving parts gives us more control, because it genuinely doesn't, no matter how logical it may sound. This doesn't matter whether you are young or old, it's a relaxed, well-coordinated, and free-flowing swish that gives us both control and length, and we can't do this from a short, tight, and controlled backswing.

Perhaps I should just add here that we're not actually focusing on swinging the club long either. In fact ideally, we're not focusing on anything in particular regarding our swing, and are simply reacting instinctively. Our swing will move into the positions that it wants to, as a natural reaction to the shot that we want to hit.

And finally, do all of the things in the book and try to change your mindset and approach towards playing golf. As your confidence improves, then so will your ability to keep your swing free of crippling and inhibiting tension.

Okay, that's just about it. This should help you to slowly regain all that youthful feeling and exuberance that you once had, so good luck with it.

ON THE TWELFTH
THE YIPS

In which we look at the golfing condition that is generally referred to as the Yips. Many people assume that this condition is confined to putting, but it can occur in any part of our game. If we can formulate a better understanding, then we are also likely to be able to find the right kind of solutions that are focused around our own particular needs.

Yes, the Yips are presently somewhat of a mystery, and can be such a huge burden, as they spoil a person's enjoyment of the game, while being potentially career wrecking for a professional. However, using *Rtf* principles, we can learn to understand them better, and then use this knowledge to be able to tackle them.

Understanding the Yips

The easiest way to understand them is to use our example of walking along the two-foot wide plank once more.

When it's just a few feet off the floor, some people

have managed fine, and some people are struggling, for a whole host of different reasons. However, as the plank is lifted higher and higher, more and more people begin to struggle. Eventually, after a certain point, everyone is clutching on to the plank for dear life, with the whites of their knuckles showing, completely frozen to the spot, and unable to move. At this point, Mr Sensitive has gone too far out of his own comfort zone, as he fears for our safety. Being the strongest one, he has entirely taken over at the helm, pushing Mr Computer to one side. He has gone into full-scale panic, and nothing will persuade him to release his stranglehold. And this is exactly the same as when the Yips have taken a permanent hold on our game. Mr Sensitive has given up all hope of being able to trust, and nothing can persuade him otherwise. Playing golf may not be life threatening, but it can really take over our emotions, and Mr Sensitive has reacted in the same way. At this point, there is no hope of any kind of fluid, coordinated, or balanced movement, just as it wouldn't be on the plank forty storeys in the air, either.

So what can we do about it?

First, we try to do the equivalent of lowering the plank back down onto the ground, just as we did when we established our starting point. We aim at nothing and try to recapture the feeling of our ten swing, without the pressure of a target.

By recapturing the feeling of our ten swing, or getting as close as we possibly can, we have at least reconnected with some kind of fluid movement, and jogged our memory of how it feels when we allow Mr

Computer the freedom to be able to do his thing. And from this point onwards, we have to give as many reasons as we can to Mr Sensitive, as to why he should begin to trust once more.

The key is to use sensible trial and error, together with the One Shot Theory. We often fail by trying to make that one giant leap, hoping to cure the problem all in one go. In other words, it's either wrong, or it is right.

If we can make some kind of headway, we must be sure to pat ourselves on the back, and look for our next chance to placate Mr Sensitive further still.

So now, we work slowly through all the things that our conscious self is responsible for, and try to slowly keep lowering the degree of difficulty, and wait for Mr Sensitive to slowly start to release his grip. Plus, of course, our conscious mind is responsible for positive and calming dialogue, which will go a long way towards our cause.

Then, just as we would do whilst trying to improve our game, we try to become more imaginative and instinctive, helping our conscious mind to slowly discard its controlling, stiff, and mechanical thinking, allowing Mr Computer back in, restoring our smaller muscles back to full working order.

As long as we are patient, in time, we will likely find ourselves better than we ever were before, as we learn so much about ourselves, which we otherwise would never have had the chance to do.

PART SIX

ON THE THIRTEENTH
FINALLY, A STEP IN THE RIGHT
DIRECTION

*In which we look at the initial compass setting as Golf
began.*

The record books say that we have been playing
golf since the year 1457. I can only assume, even then,
golf would have been a competitive sport, which
means that people would have been keen to learn,
and the better players became the teachers, just as it is
today.

Of course, much has changed since this time,
especially the courses, equipment, and technology.
However, there are two things that haven't changed at
all: at least not yet.

Firstly, all good players were able to swing with
fluid coordination and create a free flowing, non-
manipulated and uninhibited swish of the clubhead at

impact, which led on to hitting a great shot, just like they can today.

And secondly, everyone, when they began to play golf, assumed that the goal, and what they were trying to achieve, was to learn how to hit the ball straight; once again, just like they do today.

Of course, why wouldn't they? We all naturally assume this. This means that our goal then, was the same as it is today, being, both to learn, and to be taught, how to hit the ball straight. This means that from this point onwards, those that are trying their hardest to improve, will have to be checking all of the time, that everything is perfectly in position, enabling us to hit this required straight shot. Our set-up must be perfectly square, and all the positions throughout our swing perfectly on line, which will produce the perfect straight shot, that we're all constantly searching for. If we're not standing square, or swinging perfectly on plane, our friends or an instructor will be quick to point out exactly what we're doing 'wrong.'

This is probably the moment when we should ask ourselves a few rather thought provoking questions.

Is it possible, all those years back, that we took a step in the wrong direction, when we assumed that the goal was to stand and hit the ball straight, with all teaching having evolved from this initial assumption?

Do the words 'straight' and 'square' encourage us into a more robotic mentality and way of thinking, and lead us further and further away from tapping into the full power of the subconscious mind?

Did complicated technique become a part of both the learning and the teaching of golf, the instant we decided that our goal was to stand perfectly square and hit the ball dead straight?

Are these an ideal set of circumstances to be able to perform our one and only basic? A fast, fluid, free flowing swish of the clubhead through impact?

This is how Rtf sees it

First of all, we cannot try to solve problems as if we were somehow able to perform and swing like robots under clinical conditions. Not only is golf a game of almost infinite variables, but humans cannot work this way. We are full of feelings, emotions and the amazing ability of our subconscious mind; none of which can be either seen or measured.

So, our initial goal would be to create a free flowing swish, and then a good strike on the ball. Our subconscious mind would quickly learn the feel of this, just as it would learn how to throw a ball. Once we've grasped this, we begin to learn the feeling of a small fade, and a small draw, just as we would likely do when playing tennis or table tennis.

Just as it would be in these other sports, this might be one step too far for some people, but that really doesn't matter, as they can stay focused on their free flowing swish, with no need to go any further. However, for those that have higher ambitions, learning to fade and draw helps us to move away from stiff and mechanical ways of thinking, and pushes us towards being able to fully engage our subconscious mind, where we can discover our own natural, instinctive and fluid golfswing.

Under Rtf, 'straight' and 'square' is not something that is sought after, unless it is what Mr Sensitive is most comfortable with; even then there is likely to be a slight bias, one way or the other.

This won't mean that we can entirely forget technique but we will have lost almost all of the technical facts that come together with 'Straight and Square.' Under our present system, many golfers still manage to slip through the net unscathed and are able to play instinctively. However, far too many become trapped and tied up by mechanical ways of thinking, and forego the chance to discover their own true potential, whilst many can even become much worse.

With Rtf, we will have discarded 'right' and 'wrong,' and some Golf Professionals may want to adopt a new and 'softer' role, becoming mentors as opposed to teachers. Golf learning could become more natural and subconscious, making golf so much more fun to play, having lost the ever growing set of complicated instructions that are slowly suffocating so many players, and the golfing industry.

This may sound like we're settling for second best if we were to discard much of the technical and arguably more scientific approach, but I have actually experienced the complete opposite, and those golfers on the Rtf train, have flourished: more than I ever dared to wish for.

My conclusion here is that the initial 'Straight' compass setting has been the bane of golf learning since 1457. The Rtf approach has moved away from

'Straight,' and accordingly resets the compass, as we begin our journey to our own great golf: in exactly the opposite direction.

So, perhaps it's now the moment to finally bury the old ways right here, right now... teaching based on the Straight Shot, born 1457 died 2016 RIP.

SUMMING UP

I'm really hoping that I've left you with the confidence and conviction to know that this is all about you and your own journey, and you are no longer willing to do something because someone else has said that you should or have to do something; you no longer have to do anything! As a rule, anything that is likely to have any kind of positive influence on your game, will be at least relatively easy, and will show some positive results immediately. I would strongly urge people away from these mostly false promises that tell us it's going to take months of hard practice, with lots of drills, and then finally our swing will be 'correct'. My belief, and preference, is that this mostly ends in failure and we are 'never' correct; we simply are where we are, at any moment in time, and there will always be opportunities to improve, regardless of what level we are playing at.

Presently, under traditional ways of thinking, we are always concerned with what we've done wrong. To name just a few:

'We didn't complete our backswing.'

'We lifted our head.'

'We didn't follow through.'

'We didn't turn.'

Under *Rtf* thinking this no longer exists, and is replaced by, 'We didn't manage to coordinate our swing as we had intended.' And the reason for this is that Mr Sensitive was not trusting the set of circumstances he was experiencing which our conscious had presented him with. It is then our job to slowly learn all about Mr Sensitive's concerns, and eventually give him enough reasons to trust and allow Mr Computer to be able to perform at his best. By doing this, we are 'lowering the degree of difficulty' for Mr Sensitive, and giving him the chance to trust.

Just to finish off the book, here is a summary of the *Rtf* preferences.

Rtf preferences

Firstly: If you feel the need to have a swingthought, see it as a whole swing, from start to finish, and picturing yourself hitting the intended shot. This is as opposed to trying to achieve an individual position within your swing. Eventually, swingthoughts become more and more distant, much as they do when you are learning to drive a car.

Secondly: The swing itself is simply a subconscious response to the set of circumstances that have been set up by our conscious mind. For this reason, all improvement will come from only two areas. The first area is our own natural development, just like we improve at throwing a ball, the more we do it. The second area is a change in any one of the things that our conscious mind is responsible for. This is our grip, clubface angle, stance, ball position, shot picturing, decision making, and the dialogue, if any, within our own mind. Our conscious is also partially responsible for our aim, but, ideally, this is connected to the shot-picturing process, and our feel and instinct are predominant over any kind of mechanical thoughts. Aiming mechanically and entirely consciously is not a recipe for success.

Thirdly: Remember how 'curved' is compatible with our subconscious and how 'straight and square' can potentially handcuff Mr C and lead to clumsy, uncoordinated movement. Therefore, even if the desire is to hit the ball straight, there is a slight bias in our swing, one way or the other. Either that or a straight shot is simply something in between a draw and a fade, and doesn't come from an overly mechanical or exact thought processes.

Lastly: All improvement comes in small steps, and we never try to make that giant leap between wrong and right. Particularly as we now know that these two words no longer exist in any golfing vocabulary. Small steps are the only way we can maintain sustained improvement, as we learn more and more about ourselves. By making small steps, we can always keep the momentum moving in our favour.

I can only end this book in hoping that it was of real benefit to you, and was a positive experience. I truly hope that the honesty and passion with which it was written came through.

Rich.

IN THE NINETEENTH
THE AUTHOR AND HOW IT ALL
CAME ABOUT

*A very open and honest account of Richard's background
and thoughts, together with some of the encounters that led him
to where he is today.*

I earned my rights to play on The European tour
at the age of twenty, the year was 1978.

At the end of my first full year, I finished one
place behind Ian Woosnam in the Order of Merit,
and exempt from having to qualify for the following
year. An article in one of the golf magazines tipped
me to be one of the top twenty players to look out for
in 1980, next to the likes of Jacklin, Seve, Faldo and
Lyle. I was also offered free coaching with arguably
the top coach in the world at that time. All in all, not
a bad start for someone who hadn't enjoyed an
especially illustrious amateur career.

All this might sound like I was a hell of a player,
but actually I wasn't, and was definitely over achieving
at this stage, especially considering the fragile qualities

of my game. I was pretty good at scoring, and was a fairly good striker, but struggled badly with direction and often hit the ball 'all over the place.' When I heard that I was going to receive free coaching from one of the top swing gurus in the world, this really looked like, and should have been, such a great opportunity. However, things didn't work out as I'd imagined and hoped for, and instead of improving, my ball striking became significantly worse. I was sure that things would eventually turn round just as soon as my new swing had bedded itself in, but despite my best efforts there was not even a glimmer of hope and my game continued to deteriorate, which slowly turned into a long term slump. I didn't have any alternative ideas myself, so I often sought further advice in the hope that things might change, but this only seemed to make matters worse.

Of course, there were many others who didn't experience the same problems as me, otherwise the swing guru wouldn't have had the reputation that he had. However, in my case, this turned out to be the first of many other experiences, that would eventually lead towards pushing me in a different direction altogether.

It wasn't until 1987 when I would get my next, more significant, opportunity.

Completely out of the blue, I was offered a great sponsorship deal, all thanks to a good friend of mine and a fellow pro on tour. This clearly gave me a bit of an all round boost, and I went on to have a couple of half decent results on the back of it, even though I'd actually hit the ball terribly! Following on from this, in the early part of 1988, I was on my way to

Africa to play on the fantastic Safari tour, which was still a major part of our calendar back then. Suddenly I had no real financial worries, at least for the time being, and I was still feeling good about my recent results, even though the standard of my golf hadn't been that good. I can remember so clearly sitting at the airport and thinking quietly to myself, 'Why am I so worried about playing badly, when I can still achieve some pretty reasonable results anyway?' My mindset had changed, and I decided, right there and then, that I was no longer going to concern myself or feel bad about my swing or the way I hit the ball. While at the same time, somewhat inexplicably, I realised that I no longer feared the other players that were on the same trip; not even the more well known ones like Vijay and Monty. I wasn't going to practice either, as I knew this would only likely lead to worrying about my swing, and I was determined that my only focus should be 'to get the ball in the hole in as few shots as possible,' and to get the job done.

Yes, you guessed it, I suddenly started to both hit the ball and play much better. I ended up finishing 2nd in The Order of Merit, behind Vijay, and probably would have won, if I hadn't been disqualified in the very first event. Almost over night my fortunes had changed, and this was my big chance to properly break through on The European Tour. Suddenly, this looked a very real possibility.

Yes, you probably guessed right again; this mindset didn't last and I was soon back to my old habits, lacking any trust in my swing and trying to both adjust and analyse it, and my game started to slide downhill once again.

This wasn't quite as crazy as it probably sounds, because, when I returned to play on The European tour, the weaknesses in my game were highlighted once more on the different types of courses, and it was clear that I still needed to somehow learn to hit the ball with a lot more control. At that time, and arguably even now, the only way to achieve this was to improve your swing mechanically.

Despite this, I did experience some very short bursts of form every now and then, but not as a result of any swing changes. One of them happened while playing in a European tour event in France. I'd had one of those rounds where I couldn't have hit the ball much worse, but had somehow managed to shoot a respectable score of 73. After the round, a sports psychologist offered to help me on the range, after hearing how I was struggling. Within the space of about half an hour, things had changed dramatically, and I'd really begun to hit the ball fantastically. Somehow my swing had begun to feel great, even though I'd not even thought about it, or made any intentional changes to it. He was working with visualisation as a tool, and it had really changed something and worked well. The following day he walked all 18 holes with me, and this really helped me to 'stay in the moment', and true to his coaching from the previous evening. I shot a 68, hit the ball really well, and was lying 5th after two rounds. Unfortunately, once again, I wasn't able to turn this into any kind of sustainability, just as had happened before, but this experience stuck with me, and became a very useful part of my education.

NB. Actually, the way it is was back then and still

appears to be now, we are either working on mechanics with a Swing guru or our mind with a Sports psychologist. It's never a combination of the two, even though we can now see how closely connected to each other they actually are. I hope you'll agree, that the future of coaching will surely recognize them to be one and same, and no longer considered as two entirely separate subjects.

Anyway, by 1990 my confidence had begun to slip even further, and it had now gotten a stranglehold on my short game as well as the long game. There was no longer any choice, I had to stop playing, and soon after I started to work as a Club pro in Sweden.

I was lucky in many ways, because despite the obvious demise of my game, I never seemed to become disheartened or lose my passion to play and compete, so I continued to learn and gain experience, but nothing ever added up to any kind of complete picture, or anything that ever helped me to improve.

By now, I was having to face the very real possibility that it was all my own fault, and somehow I just 'didn't get it,' or I was lacking talent. However, I was starting to come across other alternative ways of thinking that were really starting to spring up amongst many of the more experienced pros. They had all somehow found fault with traditional methods, and had used their experience to put their own slant on the way we coach. I actually really liked much of what I heard, and was able to learn a lot from them, but was still left somehow dissatisfied. I used my own game as a barometer, and if that didn't improve, then there had to be something more that I needed to learn, and that hadn't happened yet. I didn't have much choice anyway, because I could never have stood behind something that didn't appear to work for me, no matter how good it might have sounded. I was a pretty tough judge too, because I wanted the opportunity to compete again, and had now become aware of the required standard out on Tour, and it was miles better than I'd previously realized. It was all or nothing, and I somehow had to become a better player than I'd ever been before, or at the very worst discover my own true potential. I always felt that the right kind of coaching principles should be able to show a clear route to how a person could continue to grow and develop, and that nobody ever became worse as a result of a lesson. I've never been comfortable with the fact that people can pay good money, and actually go backwards.

Just as it does in life, our experiences tend to push us in different directions. I had become heavily involved in the Custom fitting of golfclubs, where I'd been taught certain 'set in stone' and scientifically verified principles. They all seemed perfectly logical and reasonable, and naturally everyone religiously followed them. However, I couldn't help noticing how some of these things often didn't happen in real life situations, and neither was it particularly unusual when the result was the absolute polar opposite either. Unfortunately or fortunately, depending on which way you look at it, once I had opened this door and become aware of certain contradictions, my antennae were firmly up and I began to see this happening more and more, in all kinds of different situations, which also crossed into some of our more trusted and seemingly unimpeachable teaching principles. I began to suspect that there was another factor that we had somehow missed, and it was here that the seed was planted, which eventually grew into my understanding of our subconscious mind; at least in practical golfing terms.

As my understanding of the subconscious mind grew, I began to see the pitfalls as to why this is less likely to be accepted in the golfing world and why our teaching philosophies haven't moved on and more towards this direction.

It's easy to understand our fascination with technology and scientific data, and how the more concrete and tangible answers of mechanical coaching suit our own logic so much better. This is, as opposed to all of the blurry lines and grey areas that come together with human individualism and the infinite amount of variables within all of our subconscious minds, making this so much more difficult to entirely nail down, or become a product that we could easily market.

I'd not only seen my own game deteriorate under teaching, but many others had suffered similarly too, and this was clearly the initial catalyst that had forced me to open my eyes in the first place. However, I was now beginning to assemble some real knowledge and had spotted a weakness in the system, and was really gaining the confidence to move on to pastures new. I began to look beyond and more deeply into any kind of advice that I heard, and never accepted anything at face value. I can remember asking a really good player for some advice on putting once, who actually was an exceptionally good putter, even though he appeared to be moving all over the place throughout his stroke; 'literally!' His advice was that I should try and stay as still as I possibly could! Looking back, he was clearly putting with feel and was totally subconscious, had absolutely no idea of how or what he was really doing, and there was definitely not even the slightest attempt to remain even remotely still! However, he clearly wanted to show some kind of willingness to help me, so he told me what he thought he 'should say,' and what he had heard was the 'correct' thing to do. I started to become more and more aware of how our willingness and 'wanting to help' can so often become very counterproductive, and how extra information can so easily lead to a major 'traffic jam' within our subconscious mind. This was just one small and simple example, of so many other similar situations.

Once again, this advice would have sounded perfectly reasonable and logical, and along the lines of 'less moving parts equals more consistency.' However, it is more likely that this could become a very counterproductive swingthought, at least in the long term, as it would certainly make it harder to produce any kind of rhythmical, fluid movement, together with the obvious dangers of encouraging an 'over-awareness' of our movement.

My next big moment came while I was watching two Tour players in particular, while they were trying to earn their European tour card at the infamous and scary 'Tour school.' It was painfully apparent that neither of them were going to be successful, even before the tournament had started; their body language told the whole story, and they were extremely dissatisfied with their games. Neither of them lacked the ability, and they were both superb players with limitless capabilities, but nothing looked likely to help them this week.

As I watched these two players, it all started to

make perfect sense to me. Here were two players who were seriously underperforming, whose entire livelihood depended on their ability to improve and solve problems, and I could now see just how difficult this was for them. They were firmly stuck within the relatively small boundaries of 'straight and square,' and therefore very mechanical styles of thinking, and any potential solution looked very difficult to come by. At the same time, they appeared to be completely unaware of their own individual set of circumstances and how this had affected them. As far as they were concerned, they just happened to be swinging the club badly this particular week, and they had to mechanically fix their swing quickly, otherwise they were going to have a bad week.

Well, I didn't see it this way at all. I felt that if they'd fully understood the problem, they would have had a much better chance of pinpointing it, and quickly finding a suitable solution.

In order to explain, let's take just one of the players. He was a great player, who had won several tournaments, but was now in the twilight of his career, but still physically very capable indeed. He was the type of player who had experienced lots of high peaks together with some very deep troughs. This was predominantly down to whether he was able to drive the ball well and keep good control of his overall long game, just as it would be for many players. However, this player's troughs tended to be much lower and more long lasting than most others.

Now, this particular week was like no other week on the golfing calendar. This was 'The Tour school,' where he could earn his right to stay on The

European Tour and have a real chance to earn plenty of money. Or, he could fail and have very little chance of earning a living, by being restricted to only play in the minor events. This week was 'all or nothing', the stakes were very high, and the degree of difficulty had gone up considerably!'

Then, there was another problem. On this particular golf course, if you didn't hit the fairway, the trees and rough were exceptionally penal. In fact, so much so, that you could have almost made a special rule for the week that no one was allowed to miss a fairway, or simply put out of bounds stakes everywhere! Now, this player had had a history of somewhat temperamental driving, and this set of circumstances was less than ideal for him. Once again, the degree of difficulty had gone up another notch, and was inching him closer towards being out of his comfort zone.

Now, I'm assuming that the events leading up to this tournament hadn't been ideal either, and this would definitely have been more than enough to push him comfortably out of his comfort zone. His own Mr Sensitive had clearly said 'enough is enough', and he was no longer calm or prepared to trust. Any chance of fluid and coordinated movement was going to be very difficult, and this would have either felt like, or actually become, a 'fault' somewhere in his make-up. Either way, it's not difficult to see where it all started, and the unwanted doubt and tension had slowly seeped out and possibly even become some kind of physical manifestation.

As soon as I watched him hitting balls on the range, I knew that this was certainly the case. On the range, he was hitting the ball really well and with great control, looking as good as any other player there. He went on to tell me, that his iron play and short game weren't that bad out on the course, but his driver was going all over the place! It was pretty clear to anyone, that it was his driver that was doing the major damage to his confidence. So, he was fine on the range when Mr S was feeling calmer, but the added pressure out on the course was enough to take him over that point of where he was still willing to trust.

As we've said, if he'd fully understood the problem, the solution was likely to be very simple, rather than all of the complicated swing fixes that both of these players were looking at. Actually, technically speaking, a player of his calibre can't really 'lose his swing', as it would be so deep-rooted within his subconscious mind, that it would be the equivalent of saying he'd forgotten how to walk. However, there was no doubt that he was struggling to find his normal level of coordination, at least out on the course. He needed to find out why Mr Sensitive was now so anxious that he was no longer willing to trust, and the consequences had resulted in an inability to move fluidly, together with that loss of coordination.

His first area to look would be all of the things that his conscious mind is responsible for. As we know, this is his stance, grip, decision making and shot picturing, and to check if anything had unknowingly changed here, perhaps as a result of the tension? The better he knows himself and his own game, the easier it would have been to pinpoint any potential solution.

Checking his grip and stance should be a pretty straightforward thing to do for a player of this calibre.

His decision making and thoughts could have easily become misplaced while he was in such an anxious state, and well worth looking at.

Picturing a different type of shot may have suited this particular golf course a little better, and even made a small and positive change to his swing. It's not uncommon for one of my pupils to start playing much better by simply picturing a different type of shot. A draw or a fade would be the obvious choice, but by picturing the ball going a little higher or even lower can really help too.

If he couldn't find it here, he was left with plenty of other solutions that could have helped him to regain some confidence which could have potentially led to Mr S dropping below that threshold where he would be willing to release his grip and allow the possibility of regaining some fluid and coordinated movement.

He could have tried a different driver, for example, and one that might have given him a little more confidence. Either that, or he could even have taken his driver completely out of the bag for that week, and settled for only hitting a 3 wood. In normal circumstances, he would probably feel that this was 'failing' and somewhat of a 'cop out', which would have still left him feeling very negative, and still in a mindset that is not likely to help Mr S. However, if he had fully understood and was prepared to face the true source of the problem, he would have probably felt much better about it and understood that this was actually a great solution to help him through this particular week. It wasn't going to be permanent, and there will be plenty of time after the event to try and regain his confidence with the driver, but for the time being, this would have been a sensible business decision and with no need to feel bad or negative about anything! Also, by adopting a more positive attitude, he might have ended up surprising himself, as Mr S became influenced by his new optimism, and ended up swinging the club far better than he would have thought possible.

I should also add; is it really realistic to expect to be playing at 100% peak performance every time we play, as many golfers appear to do? Perhaps if we could all manage to lower these expectations, we would remain calmer and be able to focus more on getting the job done anyway? After all, golf is a game with a high degree of difficulty, and many of the great players win tournaments anyway, even when they're not playing at their best.

Anyway, hopefully, the understanding of the situation would have meant that his decisions and solutions could have come from a more level headed and business like attitude, as opposed to the frustrating, emotional and almost 'childlike' experience that it was. His goal would have been to find a way that might keep Mr Sensitive calmer and more trusting. Then, if he was no longer confined by right and wrong and his own natural prejudices, potential solutions would have literally become endless.

Suddenly, I realized that I was up and running myself and had a real and working concept. It wasn't a new 'secret of golf' or anything silly like that, and neither was it the end of the line in regards to knowledge and learning, but it was a real understanding of the problem and a mindset where solutions were so much more simple, and you could guarantee improvement.

This was five or six years ago, and the early stages of Rtf were now born. I knew that my own golf would now start to improve, and that's exactly what happened. I am now able to enjoy playing for the first time in my life, my swing no longer feels awful, and finding improvement is fun, interesting, inevitable, and of course more focused around my own needs and not necessarily confined within the industry's idea of 'normal.' Not only that, but anyone else that has come in contact with Rtf has experienced exactly the same thing. I can honestly say that I have never seen people improve at such a rate and to such an extent as they have done under Rtf, and they have all been established players who appeared to have hit a dead end with their game, after many years of playing. This is as opposed to developing golfers who would find improvement anyway, no matter which way of thinking or philosophy they were working under.

So, did I ever have the potential to become a great player and make my mark out on Tour? I'd have to be honest and say 'probably not', because I would have probably ridden the obstacles that were put in my way, a little more easily. And besides, the odds out on Tour are somewhat stacked against you. However, looking back it's so easy to see how I completely sabotaged myself, and why I always became worse with coaching.

First, I should mention, that I definitely wasn't the 'easy to drive' and 'dependable' type of car that Nick

Faldo was.

Anyway, the 'bug' bit me quickly, and I knew that I was going to be a pro. I was very dedicated, very hard working, very analytical, and with a belief system firmly in place that said, 'if I am able to learn how to swing the club perfectly, with the correct technique, I am going to become a great player.' Worse still, I was in a big hurry to get there. Every single part of my swing became very 'conscious' and positional, especially in the backswing, where the instructions were almost endless.

Every good player can probably relate to the set of instructions that we were presented with back then and probably even now, and would have no problem in compiling a list of somewhere between 20 - 40 different instructions, that we were supposed to do, and work on, at different stages of our development. Obviously we weren't supposed to think of them all at once, but it wasn't uncommon to have more than one swingthought, just on the backswing.

Bearing this in mind, this is my point.

If I were to focus or think about any one, let alone more than one, of these twenty plus set of instructions that we were supposed to do on the backswing, I would immediately find it 'a lot' more difficult to both swing and hit the ball well.

Then, there was the coaching, and, looking back, the problem here is actually quite obvious.

Due to a good amount of misinformation, which was plentiful back then, together with adding some of my own, I had managed to build up a less than ideal and very difficult set of circumstances to work with, which my subconscious was desperately trying to make the very best out of.

Any technical advice that I received thereafter, was given without any prior knowledge of this set of circumstances, and without taking them into account. Unfortunately, the advice didn't complement them either, and was generally at the complete opposite end of the spectrum to my own best subconscious reaction. This would have to, and did, become a clear recipe to disaster.

"In short, it wasn't the swing that was a problem, but the set of circumstances that I'd managed to surround myself in, and all I had to do was to remodel these in a way that was more suited to me and built around my own personal golfing DNA, which is exactly what we all should be doing, and a golfing recipe that will lead us all to our own true potential!"

Now, I don't want to deliberately go out to upset all the swing gurus out there, however, in this scenario, I owe it to everyone to share my honest opinion and conclusion after dedicating myself to golf for the past 45 years. But, before I do, I will say that I'm perfectly at ease with anyone that doesn't share this opinion and is on a different journey. We will always have discussions on this subject, and we are all individuals and develop differently, but my opinion it definitely is. And, after having fully experienced all possible sides of this potential debate.

My only goal, and the important part of the process, is to sling a weight at the end of a long stick towards a stationary ball and create a free flowing and fast moving clubhead at the point of impact, which is traveling in the right direction and at the required angle that will strike the ball well and in the direction that I'd intended. Any part of the swing that is outside of this 'slinging area' or impact zone is designed to make this process as easy and effective as possible, while being entirely personal to only me, and is my own best subconscious reaction to the set of circumstances that I am working within. For this very reason, I would have none or very little interest in any particular 'positions' in my swing, as they are entirely dependent on the set of circumstances that I have presented to my subconscious mind. So, any conscious and deliberate changes to my own natural swing are only likely to be counterproductive, as I use my own relatively feeble conscious mind to entirely undermine the extraordinary powers of the subconscious.'

There, I've said it, and glad I've got that off my chest!!

And finally

I really hope that this book has presented a good argument, while highlighting the weaknesses in our accepted methods of learning. Presently, our development comes from three entirely separate areas. These are golf instruction where we learn about the swing and stance, then the mental side which we learn from a Sports psychologist, followed by a Custom fitting expert who helps us with our clubs. Rtf has tried to show how all of these cannot be separated and the future of golf development is that they are all one and the same, and are clearly firmly attached and interdependent: mind, body, and clubs.

I don't believe that Rtf is the final word in regards to coaching golf, in fact quite the opposite, and now is the time when we can really learn at a rate like never before.

However, we probably could say, that the mindset and way of thinking that we have tried to portray in this book is the point that all coaching should now begin to evolve and grow out of, as opposed to 'the straight shot' as we once thought, and have been doing for the past 559 years.

Printed in Great Britain
by Amazon